TRAGEDY
AT SOUTHERN OREGON
TUNNEL 13

DEAUTREMONTS HOLD UP THE SOUTHERN PACIFIC

D1615914

Scott Mangold

Charleston — London

THE
History
PRESS

Published by The History Press
Charleston, SC 29403
www.historypress.net

Copyright © 2013 by Scott Mangold
All rights reserved

First published 2013

Manufactured in the United States

ISBN 978.1.62619.346.8

Library of Congress CIP data applied for.

CONTENTS

ACKNOWLEDGEMENTS

Many of my earliest memories involve trains. I was lucky to have two grandfathers who recognized my need for anything train-related. Gramps Mangold rode the bus home from work, and I would meet him at the end of the street just in time to watch Union Pacific's behemoth Streamliner grind up Sullivan's Gulch, always on time. Grampa Prather was on the road much of the time, selling tire tools from his panel truck. Often when not in school, I traveled his sales routes with him. Raised in a pioneer Willamette Valley family, he told me stories that taught me much of the history of the Pacific Northwest. Most enjoyable were tales about railroading, so it was surprising in later years to realize that he never told me about the DeAutremont holdup at Tunnel 13. It wasn't until college that I knew the story.

As a college chum and I returned to campus from a civic function, he asked if I knew that I'd been discussing oil and watercolor painting with paroled killer Ray DeAutremont. With other priorities, like graduation and the draft, I did not think much about the DeAutremonts at the time. I returned to civilian life in 1973, just in time to find local media very involved in the fifty-year commemoration of the holdup. Curious now about the sensational, morbid crime, I found myself eager to digest the daily DeAutremont feature segments. I became interested in other lesser-known aspects of the story and read and watched everything I could. Clearly, the young criminals could have made other choices—their later lives showed that. We learn from the past, and learning doesn't have to stop.

With appreciation and affection, I dedicate this narrative to my family and especially my grandfathers, Marty and Henry. Deserving special recognition for inspiration are Alice and Larry Mullaly and Dr. Bob Church, who spent considerable time convincing me that I could write a historical narrative. Larry and Alice, thank you for your fruitful visits to the wonderful California State Railroad Museum.

Very special thanks goes to Pat Harper and the staff of my fellow volunteers at the Southern Oregon Historical Society for encouragement, as well as to SOHS for allowing me unlimited use of information, photos and facilities. And thanks to Kathy Enright for finding volume 1 of the *State v. DeAutremont* trial text (hereafter called *Trial Testimony*)! The book would not have been possible without this access. Bob Hunter of the *Medford Mail Tribune* and *Ashland Daily Tidings* warrants similar appreciation for unlimited use of DeAutremont-related articles and photos.

Jim O'Donnell of the Smithsonian National Postal Museum gets the sleuth award for his relentless pursuit and location of the elusive U.S. Post Office Department photo album titled "Story of the Holdup of Southern Pacific Train No. 13, October 11, 1923—Capture and Conviction of the DeAutremont Brothers."

No less deserving of my recognition and gratitude are the several people who contributed materials, ideas and editing. It was your support that made this an enlightening and fun project. I thank you all.

Inspiration and encouragement: Alice and Larry Mullaly, Dr. Robert Church and Victoria Law.

Instruction and technical assistance: Bill Ainsworth.

Research, material and photos: Pat Harper, Kathy Enright, Dawna Curler and the Southern Oregon Historical Society; Robert Hunter of the *Medford Mail Tribune* and the *Ashland Daily Tidings*; Terry Skibby; Mike Yoakum; Kathryn Santos and the California State Railroad Museum; Jeff Cauthen and the Southern Pacific Historical and Technical Society; Ed Austin; Tom Dill; Nancy Dunn and the Artesia (New Mexico) Historical Museum and Art Center; John Glenn; Martin L. Hansen; Bill Hellie; Jim Kinney; Greg Lambert; Hadley Lovell; Rita McDonald and the Williamsburg (Iowa) Historical Commission; Bruce McGarvey; Noreen McGraw; Arnold Menke; the National Archives in Washington, D.C.; John Neilson; Jim O'Donnell and the Smithsonian National Postal Museum; John Paskell; Gary and

Robert Pederson; Bruce Petty; Mary and Diane Putnam; Jonathan Signor; John Signor; Ben Truwe; Francis Vandervelden, Laura Witt and the Oregon Department of Transportation; and James Williams.

Editing: Larry and Alice Mullaly, Chloe Sternola, Dana Tuley, Sheila Whitsett and Dick Moore.

Production: Dee Taylor, the wonderful magician who knows everything about using computers, and the dedicated and hardworking Aubrie Koenig, Ryan Finn and the tireless staff of The History Press.

Patience and tolerance (by no means the least important): my lovely, encouraging wife, Lori.

INTRODUCTION

On October 11, 1923, three young DeAutremont brothers held up Southern Pacific's train No. 13, the San Francisco Express, at Tunnel 13 in Oregon's Siskiyou Mountains. It turned out that there was neither a gold shipment nor anything of extraordinary value on the train. Tragically, the bandits killed three trainmen and a postal clerk before fleeing. In such a crime, the question is: did it have to happen this way? Were the carnage and loss of life necessary?

Following his capture, Ray DeAutremont, the philosopher of the gang, acknowledged the horrific nature of the crime and expressed his regrets. But when prodded, his answers sometimes seemed insincere, not as repentant as we would like. Instead, Ray rationalized that he and his brothers were victims of "the forces of cosmic development" (fate). His attitude suggested that the brothers could have done little or nothing to avoid their crime. Ironies undoubtedly bolstered Ray's beliefs: the first trainman to die at Tunnel 13 was Coyl Johnson. Three and a half years later, the DeAutremonts' youngest brother, Lee, died the same way Coyl died: a shot to the gut.

It's All in the Name

Researching the DeAutremonts is complicated by their altering of the family name. In the early twentieth century, Dantremont became D'Autremont and then DeAutremont. With spelling changes, they pronounced their name differently (*dot*-ri-mont and dee-*ot*-ri-mon). Family members changed their names back and forth; life being simpler then, this practice was not as problematic as it is today.

Twins Ray and Roy looked alike but were different from each other in most respects. Studying the family requires reading slowly enough to avoid confusing Ray and Roy. The brothers used aliases to stay a step ahead of the law. They changed so often that their names confused even themselves. If "James" was included in an alias, it probably was Hugh's—his choices showed hero worship of Jesse James. Also notable is the spelling of Brakeman Johnson's name. He usually went by his nickname, which research substantiates as "Coyl," not "Coyle."

Sadly, some refer to this episode of history as "the Last Great American Train Robbery." It was not. Any action that wastes life cannot by any stretch of the imagination be called "great." On June 4, 1924, Doc, Joe, Jess and Willis Newton removed $3 million in cash, jewelry and other valuables from a Milwaukee Road passenger train outside Chicago. In contrast, the DeAutremonts recovered no valuables, so they merely "held up" a train—it was not a "robbery."

Tragedy at Southern Oregon Tunnel 13: DeAutremonts Hold Up the Southern Pacific is a story of incredibly bad choices and brutal murders that affected many families. Why is it worth considering, you ask? Studying a crime does not mean glorifying it. Ignoring a tragedy denies opportunity to learn from it. Another irony of this story is the brothers' name. In French, DeAutremont means "the other mountain." They had alternatives and choices.

Chapter 1

THE SETTING

Stop your train with the engine cab just clear of the tunnel!
—Roy DeAutremont, 12:35 p.m., October 11, 1923

TRAIN TIME

It was another splendid Indian summer day in southern Oregon. The big "Deck" rolled along shiny rails as it pulled Southern Pacific's train No. 13, the Portland–San Francisco Express (or San Francisco Express), through Ashland, Oregon's north industrial area, over the Oak Street crossing and onto the main station track. It arrived at Ashland on time at 11:10 a.m. Although the sun already was high in the sky, SP's imposing Depot Hotel and the Siskiyou Mountains cast curious shadows across the scene.

The train stopped on the main track in front of the Depot Hotel, and passengers hurried to get off or on. A brakeman hustled to the front of the train and uncoupled the big locomotive. An Ashland "hostler" (roundhouse worker) climbed into the cab and cautiously moved the loco to the roundhouse service area so that workers could prepare it for its next assignment. At the same time, hostlers at the roundhouse finished adding

Ashland, Oregon, was the division point between Southern Pacific's Shasta and Portland Divisions. The ornate Depot Hotel, seen here looking south in the early 1900s, housed railroad offices and a restaurant. *Southern Oregon Historical Society, #scott5.*

water, fuel oil and sand to another Deck, No. 3626, and moved that to a nearby "ready track" for its outbound departure pulling train No. 13. It is not clear who—hostlers or the outbound engine crew—moved the engine from the ready track to the main track. A brakeman coupled No. 3626 to the train.

Train No. 13's inbound engineer used brakes and throttle for a smooth stop, and the wheels squealed and triggered a flurry of familiar activity. Passengers, baggage, express and mail went everywhere; pushcarts were piled high with haphazard loads that sometimes hid their operators and seemed to shuttle across the platform by themselves. As railroad workers scurried in their chores, young boys pestered passengers at train windows and on the platform, selling Lithia water from nearby springs and fresh fruit. The contrasts in dress between ragamuffins, railroaders and well-heeled travelers revealed a caste system into which everyone in the picture seemed to fit.

Train No. 13 originated at Portland's Union Station each evening at 9:00 p.m. Its published destination was San Francisco, and passengers detrained at Oakland Pier at 7:41 a.m. (second morning) and continued across the Bay on SP ferries to complete their journeys at the San Francisco Ferry Building at 8:10 a.m.

Among stops along the way, No. 13 was scheduled to arrive at Ashland at 11:10 a.m., depart at 11:30 a.m. and, after the "run up the hill," depart Siskiyou, Oregon, near Tunnel 13 at 12:35 p.m.[1] Ashland was the eastern "division point" (end) of SP's Shasta Division, and Gerber, California, was the next division point "west." Gerber is about 215 miles "west" of Ashland. In Southern Pacific's parlance, anything going toward SP's General Offices in San Francisco is considered "westbound" or "west." Anything going away from San Francisco is "eastbound" or "east." So, to railroaders, Ashland is "east" of Siskiyou station (although it is "compass-north").

On this day, enginemen going off duty turned over train No. 13 to veteran engineer Sidney Bates, age fifty-two, and his twenty-three-year-old fireman, Marvin Seng, both of Dunsmuir, California. Bates was hired on as a fireman with SP in 1894 and was promoted to engineer in 1899. During that time, he had an unblemished record: several merit awards for outstanding service and no demerits. Young Seng was hired on as a store helper in 1918 and was promoted to fireman that same year.

HISTORICAL LOCOMOTIVE SP NO. 3626

In 1917, Southern Pacific Lines placed orders for fifty-three locomotives that it designated as "F-class." Large and powerful with their ten sixty-three-inch drive wheels and 2-10-2 wheel arrangement, they were designed and built primarily for pulling freight trains. However, where grades were especially steep, like on the Siskiyou line, and when more locos became available, SP also used them in passenger service.[2] Other roads called their versions "Santa Fe" types, but on the SP's Shasta Division, railroaders stubbornly referred to theirs as "Decks," even though they sported a trailing truck and two more wheels than a true 2-10-0 Decapod.[3] Typically used with Decks were Class 100-C cylindrical or 100-SC semi-cylindrical oil tenders with 10,000-gallon water and 3,120-gallon fuel oil capacities.[4] When Baldwin Locomotive Works built SP No. 3626 in 1919, no one could have anticipated its tragic role in the DeAutremonts' bungled holdup and murder at Tunnel 13 on October 11, 1923.[5]

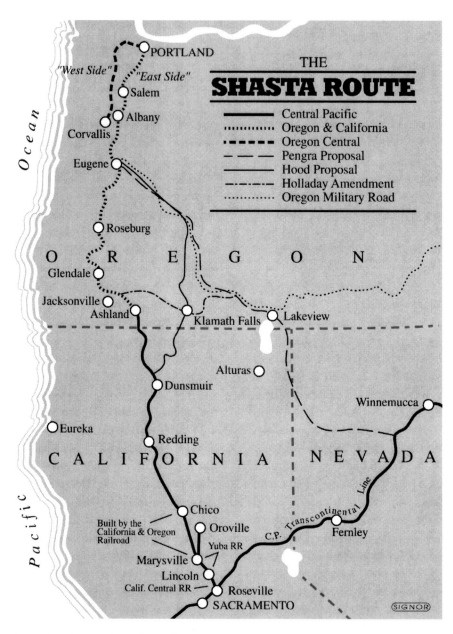

THE
SHASTA ROUTE

▬▬▬▬▬	Central Pacific
∙∙∙∙∙∙∙∙∙∙∙∙	Oregon & California
▬ ▬ ▬ ▬	Oregon Central
─ ─ ─	Pengra Proposal
▬▬▬▬▬	Hood Proposal
─∙─∙─∙	Holladay Amendment
∙∙∙∙∙∙∙∙∙∙∙∙	Oregon Military Road

PORTLAND

"West Side" "East Side"

Salem

Albany

Corvallis

Eugene

Ocean

Roseburg

O R E G O N

Glendale

Jacksonville

Ashland

Klamath Falls   Lakeview

Alturas

Dunsmuir

Winnemucca

Eureka

Redding

C A L I F O R N I A   N E V A D A

Chico

Built by the
California & Oregon
Railroad

Oroville

Yuba RR

C.P. Transcontinental Line

Fernley

Marysville

Pacific

Lincoln

Calif. Central RR

Roseville

SACRAMENTO

SIGNOR

John Signor's map of the "Shasta Route" (left) relates route proposals, actual construction and major rail points of the last half of the nineteenth century. *John Signor.* The "Siskiyou Line" (right) was that portion of SP's Shasta Division that crossed the mountains and extended several treacherous miles on both sides of Siskiyou Summit. *Ed Austin and Tom Dill.*

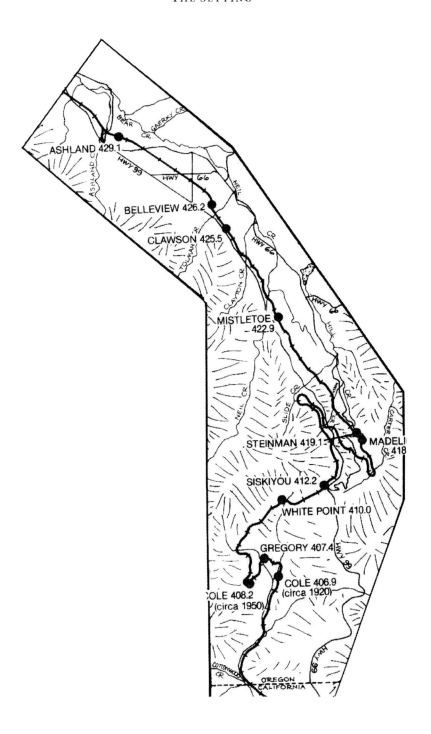

Heavy traffic during and after the Great War strained the Siskiyou Line's single-track mainline, keeping railroaders on their toes. This continued until SP opened the Cascade Line in 1926. *Southern Oregon Historical Society, #3998.*

SP loco No. 3626 pulls train No. 13, the westbound San Francisco Express, out of Hornbrook, California, in 1924. Southern Pacific called its ten-drive-wheel locomotives with 2-10-2 arrangement "Decapods," or "Decks" for short. No. 3626 (not No. 3629, as misreported) was pulling train No. 13 when it was held up by the DeAutremonts. *Tom Dill.*

SP No. 3230 and No. 3623 on the head end of train No. 13 ready to leave Ashland, Oregon, in 1924. The crew will perform a brake test and then proceed "railroad west" to grades of 3 percent and steeper. *H.L. Arey photo, Martin E. Hansen Collection.*

Brakeman Charles O. "Coyl" Johnson was hired into his position in 1917. Although deadheading this day, his role would be prominent in events. His wife, Ruby, was at home in Ashland, arranging a party for what would be Coyl's thirty-seventh birthday the next day.

Seng and Johnson both had impressive service records with no demerits.[6] There had been rumors lately that "Sid" Bates, highly regarded by all, might retire soon—a serious loss for the division and all who worked with him. Seng was disciplined and accomplished for his few years on the road—a serious railroader eager to learn.

Bates and Seng swung up through a gangway onto the cab floor. Having spent the night in boardinghouse rooms rented to the company, they stowed their grips under the cab seats. Conditioned in his routine, Seng snapped to the gauges on the left side of the boiler backhead. He knew that Bates would start asking about water, fuel, fire, steam and a dozen related responsibilities. Together, the enginemen would verify that the big loco had been lubricated during servicing.[7]

After being topped off to about ten thousand gallons in Ashland, the loco should not require more water before reaching Orcal on the California border. Seng would watch their water level and add more at Steinman, Oregon, if the loco was using more than they expected. Almost unnoticed in all the activity, another loco—a slightly smaller 2-8-2 "Big Mike" (or "Mikado") type of locomotive—backed down the station track to the front of loco No. 3626; No. 13's head brakeman, Lowell Grim of Ashland, hurried forward to "make the joint" (couple the helper to the front of No. 3626).

Adding a helper engine and crew always changed train dynamics. Helper locos were used along much of the Siskiyou line, especially from Ashland to Siskiyou and from Hornbrook, California, to Siskiyou, because of exceptionally steep grades. Above Steinman, grades exceeded 3.3 percent in places, some of the steepest on Class A railroads in the United States. Nothing about crossing the Siskiyou Mountains was easy.

In the Central Pacific (CP) Railroad's *1886 Annual Report*, Chief Engineer William Hood described the challenges of building the northern California line and crossing the Siskiyous: "The country traversed by this new road is of exceedingly formidable character, and required the most expensive class of grading in cutting the roadbed along the rugged mountain sides. The Sacramento River was crossed thirteen times with iron bridges…five tunnels were required…driven through very hard rock and under many difficulties from water and insecure material. The remaining road to be built across the Siskiyou Mountains will compare with the most expensive railroads ever constructed."[8]

CONQUERING THE SISKIYOU BARRIER

There was little surprise when the train carrying dignitaries from California to the golden spike ceremony in Ashland on December 17, 1887, was delayed several hours by weather and track problems. The Siskiyou Mountains promised early on to hinder development of southern Oregon. During the 1820s, trappers and traders of the Hudson Bay Company struggled with terrain and travel. Peter Skene Ogden convinced local Indians to show him ancient footpaths across the mountains. With the California Gold Rush of the 1840s, paths became wagon trails. In 1851, Oregon hosted its own gold rush, and traffic over the Siskiyous reversed direction. Now there was opportunity in Oregon for mining of gold and other minerals, lumbering, ranching and farming. But tapping these required transportation.

The main travel route to southern Oregon was from the Pacific Ocean to Crescent City, California, then an animal pack train to Jacksonville, Oregon. It was uncertain and dangerous. Skirmishes and then full-scale Indian wars slowed commerce and growth in the 1850s, but not for long. The Oregon territorial legislature created and franchised the Siskiyou Mountain Wagon Road Company to Michael Thomas in 1857. Within a year, Thomas and his associates had sold the franchise to trailblazer Lindsay Applegate. In 1860, the federal government granted a contract to the California Stage Company (also called from time to time the Oregon-California Stage Company and the California-Oregon Stage Company) to transport mail, passengers and freight between Sacramento and Portland. The wagon road became the primary means of transportation and communication between California and Oregon. Since operators were obliged to "maintain" the road, travel conditions improved somewhat. There remained, however, plenty of accidents, delays, discomfort…and robberies.

Because there were no reasonable alternative routes over the mountains, the toll road was profitable. In the 1860s, the Jesse Dollarhide family traveled west and started farming and sawmilling in southern Oregon. They needed affordable transportation for their businesses and talked Lindsay Applegate into selling the toll road in 1875.

Well before the 1860s, it became apparent that coastal steamers, wagons and a toll road would not resolve southern Oregon's transportation dearth. What was necessary was a rail line between Portland and Sacramento.

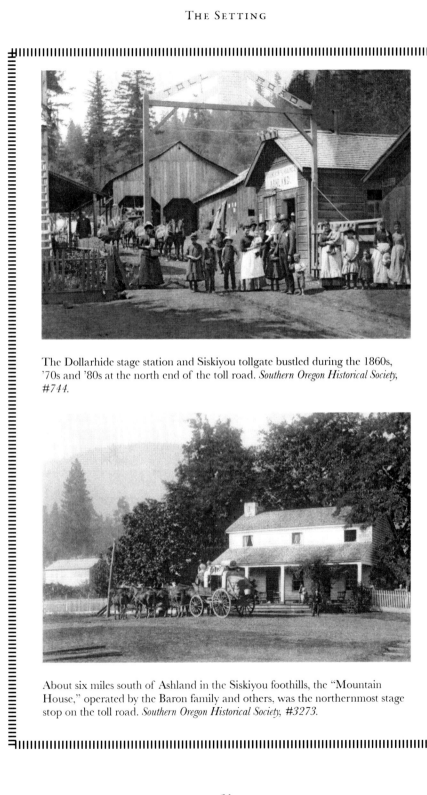

The Dollarhide stage station and Siskiyou tollgate bustled during the 1860s, '70s and '80s at the north end of the toll road. *Southern Oregon Historical Society, #744.*

About six miles south of Ashland in the Siskiyou foothills, the "Mountain House," operated by the Baron family and others, was the northernmost stage stop on the toll road. *Southern Oregon Historical Society, #3273.*

That realization attracted transportation tycoons like Ben Holladay and Henry Villard from northern Oregon, as well as the "Big Four" of transcontinental railroad fame: Charles Crocker, Mark Hopkins, Collis P. Huntington and Leland Stanford from the south. It wasn't long before entrepreneurs at both ends were surveying, buying rails and planning to meet somewhere between.

However, these were times of economic turmoil and financial challenge. Construction at both ends slowed and even stopped, sometimes for years. Reorganizing seemed to provide temporary stimulus, so laying track at different times were the Oregon Central Rail Road Company, the Oregon Central Railroad, the Oregon & California (O&C), the California & Oregon, the Central Pacific and the Southern Pacific, as well as a few predecessors of these roads.

When the SP took over management of the CP and then control of the O&C in 1884, construction resumed at both the southern and northern railheads. During the last few miles of construction, stagecoaches met CP trains to shuttle passengers, freight and mail between the Siskiyous and Ashland. With the final length of track laid in December 1887, the transportation gap was bridged.

"ALL ABOARD!"

Back in Ashland on this gorgeous fall day, train No. 13's helper was coupled onto the "point" (front of the train). Head Brakeman Grim connected the air and signal lines between the two locos and opened the "angle cock" valves so air pressure would activate the train's brake system. He signaled Bates and the helper's engineer that the connections were good. With the two locos joined now, Bates turned the valve on his brake stand that activated the "double-heading" feature.[9]

An important aspect of adding a helper to the point was that the helper engineer now was "in charge." Bates and Seng would still have plenty to do, running No. 3626 in sync with the helper engine, but until the helper was cut off at Siskiyou Station, it was the helper's engineer who would be responsible for communication and operation of train No. 13.

Seng and Bates checked their gauges again.[10] Bates verified that his "water glass" (gauge that shows that water around the boiler's "crown sheet" is sufficient to prevent catastrophic overheating and explosion) was half full. With the Siskiyou line's steep grades, he preferred to have the water level show at three-quarters on the glass, but on fairly flat stretches such as the Ashland rail yard and out to Clawson, he was satisfied to start with less water and add as necessary.

This was a run everyone knew. Engine crewmen Bates and Seng would terminate at Dunsmuir, California, before the train reached the "west" (compass-south) end of the Shasta Division at Gerber. The train crew—Conductor J.O. Marrett, Head Brakeman Lowell S. Grim, Rear Brakeman James H. Benjamin (all from Ashland) and Brakeman/Electrician/Baggage Man John Mitchell of Berkeley—would continue on to Gerber for their crew changes.

THE OTHER TUNNEL ROUTE

In 1883, O&C tunnel crews jumped ahead of grading crews and began excavating tunnels at both Siskiyou Summit and Buck Rock to the east. There being no good alternatives to a rail crossing near the summit level, plans for a tunnel there were "set in stone." That was not the case, however, with planning the route between the summit tunnel and the foothills below to the north. O&C engineers had surveyed and mapped a long reverse loop route that would lead trains through relatively gentle grades and curves and tunnels at the summit and Buck Rock.

Not everyone favored the Buck Rock route. As late as February 1887, CP's engineers sought a shorter, faster route over the Siskiyous. The route they came to favor had sharper curves and steeper grades than the Buck Rock plan and so would be more difficult to build. In its favor, this more direct route was two and a half miles shorter than the Buck Rock route, so trains could be operated for shorter distances and probably operated cheaper. The route decision fell to Chief

23

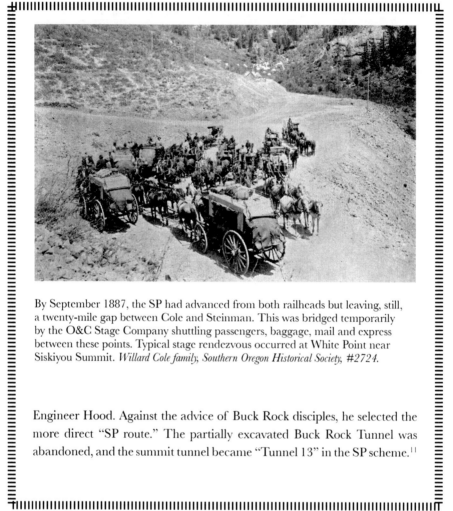

By September 1887, the SP had advanced from both railheads but leaving, still, a twenty-mile gap between Cole and Steinman. This was bridged temporarily by the O&C Stage Company shuttling passengers, baggage, mail and express between these points. Typical stage rendezvous occurred at White Point near Siskiyou Summit. *Willard Cole family, Southern Oregon Historical Society, #2724.*

Engineer Hood. Against the advice of Buck Rock disciples, he selected the more direct "SP route." The partially excavated Buck Rock Tunnel was abandoned, and the summit tunnel became "Tunnel 13" in the SP scheme.[11]

"FIRST-13" AND "SECOND-13"

Train weight that day, including fish from the north, was heavy enough to require running train No. 13 in two sections, "First-13" (1-13) and "Second-13" (2-13) trailing just a few minutes behind. Train 1-13 consisted of eight cars: a combination baggage/RPO (Railway Post Office, referred to as the "mail car"),[12] four baggage/express and three passenger cars (one coach, one chair and one all-day lunch); 2-13 pulled the trains' Pullmans.

Leaving Ashland, each section was pulled by a locomotive and helper engine. Helpers would uncouple and leave their trains at Siskiyou.

From recent experience, 1-13's conductor, Marrett, expected to depart Ashland with about one hundred passengers onboard, of which ten or twenty probably would be "non-revenue": deadheading trainmen, SP employees and pass riders.[13]

With heavy express that day, the American Railway Express Company had assigned a crew of five to 1-13: messengers Ambrose P. Bonham and Dewey Sackett and helpers Hugh Haffey, Henry B. Carter and William Radcliffe. All four baggage cars were equipped with floor racks for icing and transporting fresh fish. The mail car also had a floor rack, but fish shipments were restricted to the baggage cars. The express men said later that they kept busy icing fish that day.[14]

Mail car No. 5037 was partitioned into front and rear halves, and the mail compartment was forward, coupled to the loco tender. Although a small door allowed passage between compartments, it could be locked from the postal side. According to express messengers and helpers, the U.S. mail clerk assigned to the train, Elvyn Dougherty of Ashland, communicated little with them that day.[15] In fairness, it is likely that with the workload of many sacks of mail cluttering the car, he was too busy to visit. This was not Dougherty's regular shift. He and fellow mail clerk John Edwards often traded shifts, as they had on this day, so Dougherty could take off several days to go bird hunting.[16] Looking at all the mail sacks, Dougherty may have regretted his day trade.

Two or three minutes before scheduled departure time (11:30 a.m.), Conductor Marrett called out loudly in a commanding voice, "All aboard!" He and Rear Brakeman Benjamin hustled the last passengers onboard, secured the plates over vestibule steps and closed the side doors. Then Marrett stood tall and waved his arm to give the "highball" signal to the engineers. The helper loco's engineer (in charge now) reached for the cord and acknowledged the conductor with two long whistle blasts.

The helper engineer turned on his bell—for safety, it was to sound as long as the train was moving and people were in the area. Bates and the helper engineer pushed their "power reverse" gears all the way forward for maximum steam and power. Double-heading, Bates had no control over the train brakes, but he released his engine brake and began to slowly open his throttle. As No. 3626 inched forward, it gently pulled the slack out of the couplers and then nudged the helper's tender. When the helper's engineer felt the "boot," he opened his throttle. Passengers always appreciated a smooth

Left: U.S. Mail Clerk Elvyn E. Dougherty poses in happier times on the porch of his Ashland home with wife, Blanche, and son, Raymond. Dougherty would be the first to die in the Tunnel 13 holdup. *From the Ashland Daily Tidings, September 30, 1976.*

Below: SP 5036, Pullman Class 60-BP-30-1 postal-baggage car, was a near-identical "sister" car of O&C 5037, the target of the DeAutremont brothers' holdup. *A.C. Phelps photo, Jeff Cauthen Collection.*

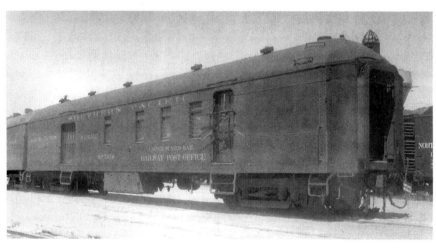

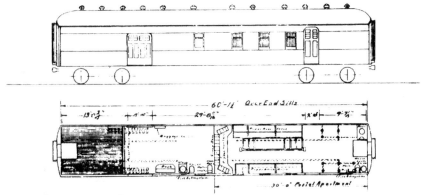

Drawings show the mail car's provisions for lighting and heating. The mail compartment is shown to the right. *From the Southern Pacific Historical & Technical Society's* Diagrams, Common Standard Passenger Train Cars Southern Pacific Lines as of March 1, 1933, *Southern Pacific Historical & Technical Society and Jeff Cauthen.*

Two helper locos descend the grade at the Steinman overpass while a motorist watches. A construction feat in its day, the Pacific Highway was both functional and majestic. *Terry Skibby.*

start, and Bates was a master. The train began to move at 11:34 a.m., four minutes late, to Conductor Marrett's chagrin.[17]

The next order of business was the "running brake test." The SP Rule Book required that the forward engineer administer a brake test whenever the engine crew or motive power changed (as with adding or cutting off a helper). So, running brake tests were required at both Ashland and Siskiyou. The Ashland test was uneventful, but following the Siskiyou test, life would change for many families.[18]

Skilled mechanics, the enginemen hastened to their routines. The sounds, smells and movements of locomotives and crews working together were exactly as they should have been. It was the fireman's job to deliver proper steam to the engineer, who, in turn, used his power reverse gear, brakes and throttle to manage the locomotive's movement. Enginemen communicated even without words. An engineer could make life a living hell for a greenhorn fireman if he chose to. But not today, not these men; both engineers concentrated on their controls. The train picked up speed as it rolled south through the farms and ranches

STATIONS AND DEPOTS

Over the years, Southern Pacific designated a number of "stations" along the Siskiyou line. A station is a location of railroad activity that has purpose but not necessarily buildings or staff. Sometimes a station is little more than a siding or spur used for railroad construction or private industry (e.g., sawmills or rock quarries). If there are railroad buildings and staff at a station, it is known as a "depot."

A "train order station" is used to control capacity and congestion problems, usually on busy single-track lines. It is staffed by an operator who can stop trains and control them through the use of train orders. Troop train congestion in 1918–19 led to adding stations at Foliage and Viaduct in 1921. Train order stations must have an identifying name, a siding for trains to pass and communication between the operator and trains (signals and train orders).

Many stations were short-lived—none as short as Madeline, which is where the scuttled Oregon & California Buck Rock route would have rejoined the Ashland line only two-tenths of a mile from Steinman. When Chief Engineer Hood selected the SP-touted direct route, Madeline

The young crooks drove their auto off the Pacific Highway and camouflaged it so they could explore the Cottonwood Valley and plan their crime. *Oregon Department of Transportation.*

The Pacific Highway high above Cottonwood Creek. The State of Oregon built its portion of the grand Highway mostly between 1913 and 1915. *Oregon Department of Transportation.*

became available for naming a station on SP's Wendel/Lakeview branch line.

Over the years, names were added to and deleted from the station list, structures were removed and depots became stations or lost all status. In late 1923, stations on the "east" side of the Siskiyous were Ashland, Clawson, Mistletoe, Steinman, Foliage, Wall Creek Spur, Viaduct and Siskiyou. Ashland, Steinman and Siskiyou also were depots at one time.[19]

of the upper Bear Creek drainage and Siskiyou foothills.

Few phrases describe the diverse beauty of southern Oregon's Siskiyou country. Small, well-formed volcanic buttes reveal its geological history. Dozens of small creeks trickle through the foothills into Bear Creek on its way north to the Rogue River. Small stands of ponderosa, thickets of Madrone and mistletoe-laden oaks complement hillsides and meadows covered with tall, golden grass during these dry months. Turkey vultures and red-tailed hawks, plus an occasional eagle, circled overhead, teaching their young to hunt and survive.

Passengers and crew couldn't help but note the changes to this scene during the years they'd been riding the Siskiyou line. Transportation improvements removed obstacles to commerce and development. Looking out train windows, old-timers could remember the Applegate/Dollarhide toll road and its use by the California Stage Company. The railroad basically followed the route of the toll road, except that it was longer length to avoid the toll road's steeper grades. Between 1913 and 1915, portions of the old toll road were merged and became the route of the new "Pacific Highway" in southern Oregon. As the train sped alongside the Highway, passengers marveled at how a rutted, muddy road had become a sixteen-foot-wide ribbon of pavement extending 1,600 miles from Canada to Mexico. Now anyone could speed across the Siskiyous.

Those on the train looked down toward the "Mountain House," an old stage station, and to Barron's Ranch just beyond. With automobiles darting through the scene, the Pacific Highway was a beehive of activity. No one seemed to pay attention as these machines sped ahead of the train.

The grade grew steeper between Dollarhide and Foliage. The two engineers worked their throttles to control slack in the couplers and prevent lurching. Bates was one of the Shasta Division's best "hoggers" (engineers), but it was approaching time to turn over the rails to younger men. Wheels

Three locos pull the heavy, westbound train No. 13 over massive Wall Creek trestle, circa 1915–25. *Terry Skibby.*

squealed as the train negotiated "hairpin" curves and passed through short Tunnel No. 15 and curving Tunnel No. 14. The helper engineer pulled the whistle cord and held it. How many times had they slowed for a deer in Tunnel No. 14? The enginemen may have wondered what makes a deer go into a spooky black hole like that. They slowed as the train approached the

Siskiyou Station looking north. Over the years, several turntables served helper engines at Siskiyou. *Southern Oregon Historical Society, #2320.*

massive Wall Creek steel trestle. Bates seemed to never tire of looking down the mountainside where the track looped and reversed its direction twice. Now Siskiyou was just minutes ahead.

SISKIYOU STATION

Tracks and structures suggested a lot of railroad activity in this little mountain town. A turntable, an important tool, was used to turn around helper engines "returning light" (going back without a train). If enginemen didn't have to turn around on their cab seat, they could see better where they were going. Also, "running forward" reduced tendency for "trucks" (wheel sets) to derail. With Tunnel 13 at the line's summit, it was necessary to return helpers to both Ashland and Hornbrook. As locomotives grew in power and

Above: Siskiyou operator Bowman, station staff and a mongrel pose on a beautiful winter morning. *Southern Oregon Historical Society, #2089.*

Left: An eastbound passenger train crawls toward a Siskiyou hotel and the station beyond. *Southern Oregon Historical Society, #1602.*

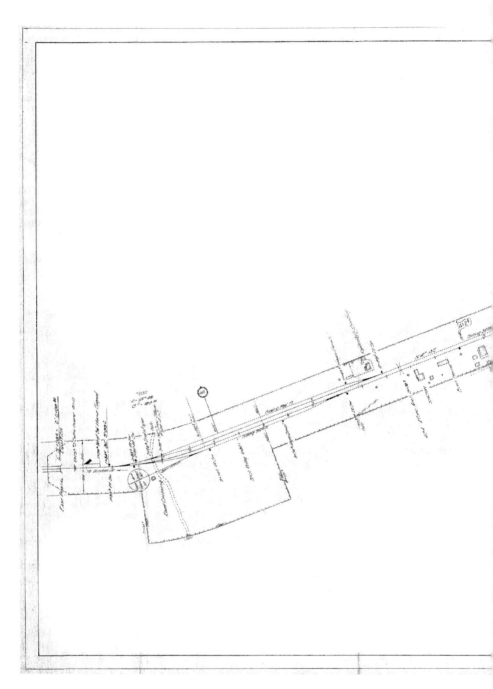

A 1920 drawing of SP's plan to fence Siskiyou offers details of the tiny station. *SP Shasta Division Archives.*

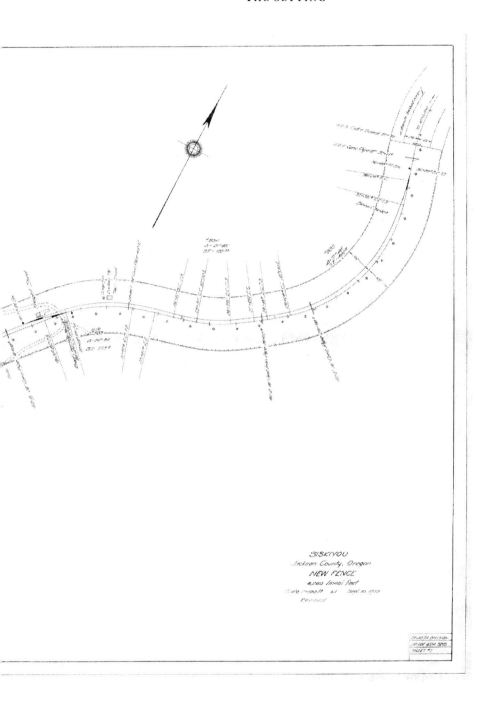

SISKIYOU
Jackson County, Oregon
NEW FENCE
6,060 lineal feet

size, it became necessary to replace Siskiyou's turntable every few years: the original forty-footer in 1887 was replaced by a sixty-five-footer, then an eighty-footer and finally a one-hundred-footer in 1922. The Siskiyou turntable was located just a few yards from Tunnel 13's east portal and on the south side of the tracks.

SP documents show that between 1920 and 1923, several yard tracks were installed at Siskiyou. Tracks were moved often, and at one time, eight tracks could be counted side by side near the turntable: "braking power," passing siding, "main track" and five helper and turntable lead tracks. The "braking power" track was used for storing empty freight cars (probably stock cars) that could be added into long downhill trains to supply extra braking effort. This short section of track at Siskiyou soon would play a significant role in history.

High in the mountains, Siskiyou was a busy place. Beyond the right-of-way were residences and commercial buildings ranging from hotels and restaurants to "entertainment" establishments. Before the Pacific Highway, Siskiyou families had to rely on the railroad to get children to and from schools in Ashland. But with the Highway opening in 1915, school buses became the safer option for transporting children to school.

Although it bustled with purpose and energy, Siskiyou was an enigmatic little settlement. It almost had the feel of a prison: secluded, wooden boardwalks and rolls of wire fencing. The fencing was mostly for controlling animals, keeping them, where possible, from going where they should not go. Then there was Tunnel 13, a 3,108-foot hole in the mountain.

Approaching Siskiyou, the two engineers eased their throttles closed and brought 1-13 to a stop in front of the tiny station. A few passengers, mostly company employees, got off or onto the train. Lead Brakeman Grim hustled forward to uncouple the helper. He closed the angle cocks on air and signal lines and lifted the cut lever. As the helper began to inch forward, the couplers and air hoses separated. The helper hissed as it maneuvered to be switched off the main and onto a storage track. It would be turned and run back to Ashland after Sections 1 and 2 passed. With the helper "cut loose," 1-13 was Bates's train now.

Chapter 2

THE DEAUTREMONT FAMILY

The Journal joins in the hearty congratulations, hoping that happiness, health and all the best blessings in life may fall to their lot.
—*"A Charming Wedding,"* Williamsburg [Iowa] Journal Tribune,
November 12, 1897

IOWA AND BEYOND

An unlikely place for a crime to spawn was the village of Williamsburg, Iowa, in the last years of the 1800s. Those involved were not bloodthirsty desperadoes but rather members of the loving family of Paul P. and Isabella "Belle" Wombacher Dautremont.

Williamsburg was neither the first nor the last frontier settlement to face ruin because a railroad changed its mind. In 1854, Welshman Richard Williams built a sawmill and platted a forty-acre townsite nearby that he named for his family. But the Rock Island Railroad reneged, rerouting and passing Williamsburg ten miles to the north. Other towns bypassed by railroads often gave up, and residents moved away, but not Williamsburg. Immigrants from Wales, Ireland, Scotland and Germany worked hard to prosper and keep their new town alive. Thirty years later

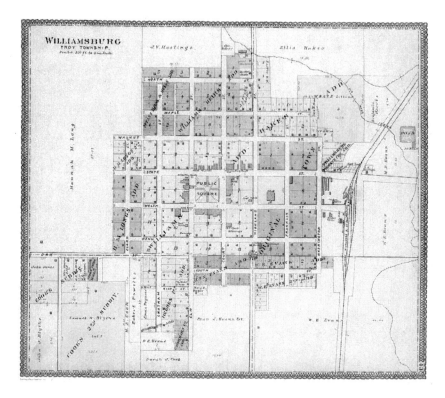

Williamsburg, a charming little village in southeastern Iowa, was founded in 1854. It was the home of the DeAutremont family, three sons of whom would be labeled train robbers and coldblooded killers in years to come. *Williamsburg Historical Commission.*

in 1885, the Milwaukee Road announced that it would locate its new line along the east side of Williamsburg. Almost overnight, the town's optimistic populace burgeoned from 150 to 1,000 residents, and the town incorporated in 1885.[1]

Paul and Belle were not newcomers; their families had lived in or around Williamsburg and Riverside (thirty-five to forty miles southeast of Williamsburg) for many years. As noted in the introduction, studying family histories can be complicated when records show a variety of name spellings. Paul's grandfather was Louis or Lewis Dautremont or Dantremont. He was a farmer born in New York, and he, wife Hanna Magee (or Hannah McGee) and their young family lived in Pennsylvania and Ohio before coming to Iowa in the mid-1800s. One of their several children, Charles Joseph (Paul's father), spelled his name both ways.

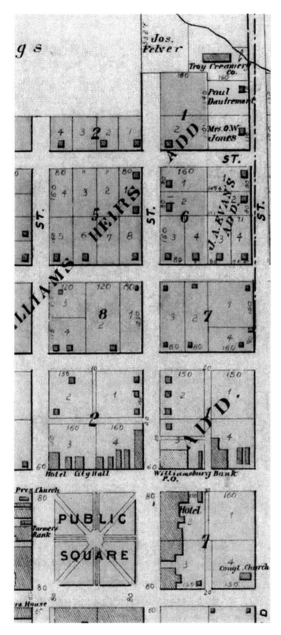

Detail: Paul and Belle DeAutremont lived in an attractive bungalow four blocks north of the Public Square. Paul's barbershop was across the street in the bank. *Williamsburg Historical Commission*.

Documents show that Charles was a "merchant," probably a shopkeeper.

Paul was born near Williamsburg in 1873. In his youth, he spelled his name as Dautremont for a while, but as a young man, he changed it to DeAutremont ("dee-*ah*-tre-mont). Isabella (Belle) was born in 1874 in Riverside, where her family had a large home. Her father, Andrew Wombacher (or Wambacher), emigrated from Germany to Iowa in the 1860s; her mother, Mary Sherer, came from Alsace or France about the same time. Although Belle's family were farmers, newspaper clippings mention travel and visits that suggest a comfortable lifestyle.

The 1920 federal census illustrates the confusion over names: it lists four of Paul's and Belle's sons as Ray and Hugh Dautremont and Charles and Verne DAutremont. Misspellings like Dellutremont also show up in records.

Paul and Belle were married in November 1897. He was a successful barber with a shop ("The Columbia") next door to the post office in the

Paul DeAutremont's barbershop was located next to the post office in the Williamsburg Savings Bank. *Melanie Landa.*

Williamsburg Bank building. A four-block walk from his shop, their attractive little bungalow was on North and Highland Streets, next door to the creamery.

Not uncommon in the age, the *Williamsburg Journal Tribune*'s wedding story painted a flattering picture of the young couple.[2] It described Paul as an industrious young man of good habits and Belle as amiable and accomplished with a wide circle of friends. Paul was active in raising and showing poultry, and Belle may have shared the hobby with him. Paul organized events during town functions. An avid foot racer for years, he later would inspire his sons toward athletics. Belle was known to host fine

ladies of the town to old-fashioned rag sewing bees in her home. Paul evidently had a flair for decorating: the *Journal*'s wedding article reported that he furnished their home before the marriage. In years to come, he'd supplement his barbering income with wallpapering and painting.

Practicing Catholics, Paul and Belle wasted no time starting a family. Belle gave birth to her first child, Paul "Verne," on January 1, 1899, and then to twins Raymond Charles and Roy Andrew on March 31, 1900. Fourth son Hugh Augustus was born on February 21, 1904, after the family moved to Mena, Arkansas. Fifth son and last child, Joseph "Lee," was born in Colorado in 1907.

Footraces were exciting and popular in little towns like Williamsburg. Paul was a splendid runner and rarely missed a race. *Bullers family.*

Mena is a scenic little town in western Arkansas' Ouachita Mountains. Nothing definitively explains why Paul moved his family across three states to Mena during or just after March 1902, but his career may explain the move adequately: larger than Williamsburg, Mena offered more opportunity for a barber. Influencing Paul's decision could have been Mena's warmer climate and handbills promoting this attractive area. He may have decided, "This is the place!" A newspaper clipping suggests that Belle liked Mena: "Mrs. Paul Dautremont writes an interesting letter to the *Riverside Leader* from Mena Ark. She likes the country, its climate is ideal and fruit grows down there in great plenty. She says that one of her hens has raised the third brood of chickens since last December."[3]

With Hugh's birth, Belle now had four preschoolers to care for—ages five, four (twins) and a newborn. Since she and Paul tried to be good Catholics, the children were christened and began religious training early in life. Belle's faith gave her great strength in dealing with challenges, and she would have challenges. About six months after Hugh's birth, Paul was ready to move again, attracted this time by the gold fields of Colorado.

Paul moved the family to Cripple Creek during the summer of 1904, and they would stay in Colorado until 1909. Paul did well in Colorado. He still worked as a barber and traveled the gold field towns in that profession, but he also took odd jobs wallpapering and painting. Decorating turned out to be lucrative.

Also significant during these years was that the boys, growing older, began to form lasting memories and impressions. In later years, Roy reflected on the lawless gold field towns and how men and children had to be tough to survive. It was hard to behave well because there was no tolerance of "sissies." Ray developed an interest in dynamite. He would steal it from gold mine supply shacks, light and throw it into ravines just to hear the terrific noise it made. Not a good omen for an eight- or nine-year-old boy.

Paul was pleased with his good fortune in Colorado, but he grew concerned that the tough environment of the gold fields was making it a difficult place to raise children. He and Belle were bothered that there were few Catholic parishes or priests nearby to tend to the family's spiritual needs. Paul began to think about another move.

In 1909, he came across handbills promoting land development around Lakewood, New Mexico, about sixty miles south of Roswell, a good-size town. He immediately fell for the green valleys, abundant water and sumptuous beauty depicted in the flyers. He was so overwhelmed by the opportunity that he sold everything in Colorado and bought land sight-unseen from a promoter in New Mexico, a Mr. Fairchild. Paul bought a covered wagon and team, loaded the family and their remaining possessions into the wagon and headed south toward Roswell and Lakewood.[1]

The sight of Model-Ts speeding past a covered wagon may have entertained folks along the way, but there was no entertainment for the Dautremonts over the eight-hundred-mile trip. They endured biting cold, snow in the Rockies, rain and furious sandstorms through New Mexico. Belle put on a tough face, but she was miserable trying to tend the needs of baby Lee and five-year-old Hugh. The older boys walked most of the distance. Water and food ran out near Roswell. The horses were so affected by the arduous trek that they would never be the same. Roy later described one horse as "ruined." Christmas was approaching, and Paul decided that they'd spend the holiday in Roswell, resting, and continue to Lakewood afterward. There had been a little snow, and this would give it time to melt.

The exhausted family was surprised to see the town hosting a Christmas footrace—in the middle of winter! This was more community celebration than they were used to, even on a Fourth of July in Iowa. Paul never missed a footrace and quickly entered this one. He won handily, beating some of the best New Mexico runners. Thereafter, locals called him the "Colorado Race Horse."

After Christmas, the family drove the wagon the last sixty miles from Roswell to Lakewood. Their great anticipation turned to shock, as "Lakewood" was nothing more than a piece of arid desert. Clearly, Paul had been badly swindled by the promoter Fairchild. Imagining the family's misery, one has to question Paul's leaving a lucrative decorating business in Colorado, loading his young family into a wagon and setting out on a perilous journey in the dead of winter. Whether driven by wanderlust or seeking a better life for his family, Paul put them in danger, jeopardizing their safety, health and what little they had.

Seeing his father discouraged and demoralized, Ray experienced the first bitter frustration he would remember later. He quickly developed hatred for anyone who tried to hurt or humiliate his family. Etched into the memory of a nine-year-old, he never forgot the Lakewood disappointment. This episode also opened a period of argumentation between Paul and Belle that was very disturbing to their young boys.

A FAMILY BREAKS UP

Paul looked at the bleak desert surrounding them and felt nothing short of abject failure. However, Belle, in her characteristic optimism, wanted to stay and make the best of their ill fortune. Paul had lost most of his money to Fairchild and others who took advantage of this newcomer family.

Seven miles west of Lakewood, the Gossett Farm was available for rent. On it was a small artesian well, and Belle convinced Paul to rent the property and try farming. The family worked their fingers to the bone raising meager crops. Success was elusive. What jackrabbits and the neighbors' cattle didn't eat would be taken to town for sale. But after "commission men" (brokers) charged Paul for transportation and other "expenses," there was nothing left. At the same time, cattlemen whose animals were dying of thirst and hunger tried everything they could to discourage settlers and coax Paul to leave so they could get his water and range grass. Paul and his sons put up sturdy wire fences, but during the night, cowpunchers would pull out the staples so that cattle could race to water and grass. Paul phoned the cattlemen to remove the thirsty beasts, but they told him to "go to hell or leave!" Paul taught the older boys—the twins nine or ten now—how to use rifles and shotguns. At night, they would ride along the fences, looking for anyone trying to damage them. It was miraculous that no one was shot. Roy grew bitter, but as a young boy, he was helpless to change his family's plight.

Fighting dangerous circumstances, Paul and Belle argued over what to do. They finally agreed to give up the farm and move into town. Belle had received an unexpected small inheritance, and it allowed them to buy a store.[5] Relationships with the "enemy" cattlemen actually improved over time, and after two years, it looked like the Dautremonts might make a go of the store. That was not to be, as the area's economy was declining rapidly. In later accounts, Roy attributed the slump to crooked promoters like Fairchild. As farmers and ranchers lost their property and townspeople their businesses, folks packed up and moved away. Paul, soured by promoters, cattlemen, crop middlemen and now the failing store, wanted to go back to Colorado. His embitterment was leading to a rift in this close-knit family, and separation seemed inevitable.

Again, Belle argued that things weren't so bad; she wanted to stay in Lakewood. More frequent verbal fighting became physical. On one occasion, Paul knocked down Belle, and she had him arrested. Out of jail and humiliated, Paul left the family and moved to Victor, Colorado, about four miles from where they had lived in Cripple Creek. A short time later, they seemed to reconcile. Belle leased out the store and took the boys to Victor to be with their father. This accommodation lasted about two years until Belle decided that she really didn't like Colorado and would return to Lakewood. Paul, it was said later, could not stand to be separated from the boys and made one more effort to reconcile. He returned from Colorado to Lakewood and bought a farm on credit. But with commission men still cheating farmers, the family found itself working for nothing again. Violent quarreling between parents returned.

At sixteen, Ray found life boring after the "cattle wars." Having had enough of his parents' bickering, he left home to explore the vast country. Roy followed shortly afterward and knocked around Colorado, Kansas and Oklahoma. Roy especially had been eager to leave home, but he found new worries. He felt puny, as he did not have the strength or stamina to tackle great challenges or accomplish much. He felt that he could not do a man's work. But then came comfort in familiarity when he saw a sign on an Oklahoma City street reading, "Barber College." From watching his dad barber for most of Roy's sixteen years, he knew that he could learn the profession.

He contacted Ray, who happened also to be in Oklahoma City at that time, and he talked Ray into joining him at barber college. They did not room together for fear of Paul tracking them down easily. The barber school made them a deal to help with tuition, and they worked as boardinghouse waiters to cover living expenses.

It felt as if things were working out, but suddenly Roy had a new problem: while attending barber school, his eyes began to bother him, and he felt that he was losing his eyesight. Ray, in the meantime, found barbering too tedious, too confining. He'd been cooped up, and now he was ready for travel and adventure. But before Ray could leave town, the twins heard from Belle that she and Paul had "serious trouble." He had left her, and she needed one or both twins to come home and help take care of the family. Ray changed his plans and found his way back to Lakewood. He would not stay long, maybe six months.

DeAutremont: "The Other Mountain"

Paul was through with his marriage, finally giving it up. Maybe he could find another life in Colorado or farther out west, he reasoned.

Aside from Roy's worries that his eyesight might fail him, he was doing well in barbering. Toward the end of his schooling, an acquaintance from Texola, Oklahoma, offered him a job, and he accepted it. But then a friend from barber college wrote to him about a better job in Lawton, Oklahoma, the closest point to Fort Sill and Camp Donovan during the Great War. He eagerly grabbed it. This job and the war led to a number of military-related barber jobs for Roy, including opening his own shop in the Seventy-eighth Field Artillery at Fort Sill.

One opportunity in the Student Army Training Corps could help him avoid the draft. However, the corps required more education than Roy had, so he resolved to work more schooling into his life. He attended high school in Lawton (but didn't graduate) and the Normal School there for one year. He also attended high school in Salem, Oregon, for a short time.

Roy had not been home to Lakewood since running away in 1916. As the war wound down in November 1918, Belle wrote again, asking that Roy come home. With barbering slowing down, he did return to Lakewood, but only for about six months. He knew that he could not make a living in Lakewood, and nearby Roswell proved no better. His meager thirty-dollars-per-week earnings after living expenses didn't go far enough in helping Belle keep Hugh and Lee in school. Discouraged, Roy returned to Lawton and put in a shop at the First Field Artillery at Fort Sill. Earning ten dollars per day, he was much more able to help Belle and the boys than if he had stayed and barbered in Roswell. Two thoughts were prominent in the letters he wrote around this time: his failing eyesight and devotion to his Catholic faith.

Ray was a bitter young man when he first took to the rails in 1916—bitter for the Lakewood experience, bitter about the "bastards" who could care less about a hardworking family trying to survive and discouraged after listening to his parents fight for sixteen years. Through his experiences, Ray's resentments intensified, and his anger grew. Similar in some ways, a major difference between the twins was that Roy had a stronger and more pious religious conviction than Ray. Unfortunately, Roy's positive attitudes would not survive.

The social face of America had been changing during the two decades from 1890 to 1910. By 1918, periods of economic turmoil, unemployment and hunger gave rise to strong pro-labor, anti-capitalist movements. Riding the rails and living in hobo camps, Ray was exposed to very different people and ideas. His weak education and lack of job, purpose and promise made him the perfect target for recruiters of "Big Bill" Haywood's radical labor movement the Industrial Workers of the World (IWW, or "Wobblies"). Their tactics involved disrupting life in the cities and then organizing the "underclass" of unskilled and migrant workers. The core of their rhetoric and actions was class warfare. They were branded socialists, communists and anarchists—whatever they were called, they were feared and despised by those who lived comfortably. It was the duty of every "good American" to help wipe out these wild-eyed Bolsheviks.

Haywood, seditious and inciting, pandered to the downtrodden, the growing legions of poor and oppressed. Ray identified strongly with the Wobblies' theme of justice for the little man, the working stiff. He felt that he had tolerated cruelty and injustice for years. Ray had only eight years of schooling and had successfully avoided books most of his life. But now, talking and listening to others as they seemed to describe his frustrations and resentments, he began visiting reading rooms and reading all he could. Books were bringing him answers and ideas that made sense. Although the IWW peaked in about 1917 and began to wane after the Great War, Ray had become an ardent believer and would regard himself a social philosopher for the rest of his life. With Ray's radical ideas and Roy always ready to follow him, the boys became known in logging camps as the "boy orators of the tall timber."[6]

After leaving home and drifting around the western United States during the war, Ray sometimes followed his dad and Paul's new wife, Nellie Mae Guard Carter, as they moved around Wyoming, Idaho and Oregon, searching for their new life. In marrying Nellie, Paul acquired an "instant family": stepchildren Ivan and Inez Carter (twins) and nephew Frank Case. Toiling among coal miners and laborers—many bitter—Ray became more and more a disciple of the IWW. He neither advertised nor hid the fact that he was a Red Card carrier: a full-fledged member of the IWW. But tired of the coal fields, he searched for better work, and in 1918, he found a job in a Vancouver, Washington shipyard, just across the Columbia River from

THE RATTLER 23

1923

RATTLER

VOLUME III.
PUBLISHED BY THE SENIOR CLASS OF THE ARTESIA HIGH SCHOOL,
ARTESIA, NEW MEXICO

Opposite: The DeAutremont family lived above their small grocery store in Lakewood, New Mexico. *U.S. Post Office Department.*

Above: The DeAutremont brothers received some schooling from the Lakewood public school. Hugh was the only brother to graduate from high school. *Artesia (New Mexico) Historical Museum and Art Center.*

Left: Hugh graduated from Artesia High School in 1923. Teachers and students agreed that he was bright, popular and involved, especially in sports, as photos show. *Bruce Family, Southern Oregon Historical Society, PAM A6, 1923.*

Portland, Oregon. Before taking the Vancouver job, Ray visited Paul and Nellie at their Salem, Oregon home.

The war ended. A year later, on November 11, 1919, the new American Legion Post in Centralia, Washington, put on the town's first Armistice Day Parade. Patriotism abounded, and all buildings were draped with American flags except one, the IWW hall. As the marching Legionnaires approached the IWW hall, they suddenly stopped. What happened next has been argued about for years. Shots were fired, and three Legionnaires fell dead in the street. The Legionnaires rushed the hall, and IWW member Wesley Everest, himself a veteran, tried to escape out a back door. He shot and killed his nearest pursuer before being captured and thrown into a jail cell. That night, the city's electricity mysteriously went off. When it was restored, Everest's body, riddled with bullets, was found hanging from a nearby bridge. Eight IWW members were jailed, inspiring a witch hunt that resulted in one thousand men and women being arrested on a variety of flimsy charges by the end of the week.[7]

There is disagreement as to how involved Ray was with the Wobblies. A longtime suspect, police officers and detectives stormed and searched his rented room in Vancouver a few days after the Centralia incident. They claimed to have found a considerable quantity of IWW promotional materials, proving that Ray was an "organizer." He argued that he had only a cartoon and was not an organizer, just a card-carrying member. He was arrested and charged with a controversial new crime, "criminal syndicalism," which made it illegal even to carry IWW identification. Ray was convicted and held temporarily at the Clark County Jail. Not helping his plight was a botched escape attempt just a few days after he was jailed. It was little more than a half-hearted effort to trick the guards. Ray and a cellmate studied the guards' routines then tried to blend in with others to sneak out. Unfortunately for them, the cellmate dropped a stack of trays, panicked and ran. They were back in their cells in minutes. Following that, Ray's last days in the Clark County Jail were hell. Because Ray was young and jailers thought him malleable, they tried to coerce him to "finger" other IWW members. When Ray refused to play stoolie, jailers tried psychological abuse to get information. Ray did not cooperate and would serve full term after sentencing.

As fraternal twins, Ray and Roy always were close, regardless of what they did or did not agree on. When Paul, living in Salem then, learned of Ray's "crime" and conviction, he frantically contacted Roy, imploring that he come north for Ray's sentencing. Roy didn't hesitate. He sold his

THE RATTLER '23

BERTHA SHATTUCK

"Minerva", Senior Play.

"A woman who can think to keep a date or promise."

HERMA WELSH

Basketball 1922 and 1923.
Chairman Home Economics Dept.
Dramatic Club.
"Marjorie", Senior Play.

"O, ye fickle bird of bright feathers!"

VESTA FRISCH

Operetta.
Assistant Editor Rattler, 1923.

*"Forever foremost in the ranks of fun,
The laughing herald of the harmless pun."*

HUGH DEAUTREMONT

Football 1923.
Captain Basketball, 1923.
"Richard", Senior Play.
Athletic Editor Rattler, 1923.
President of "A" Club, 1923.

"An optimist in the guise of a pessimist."

Hugh's activities during his senior year included membership on the yearbook staff and in the drama club, being president of the lettermen's club and being active in football, basketball (as captain) and track. *From the* Carlsbad Argus.

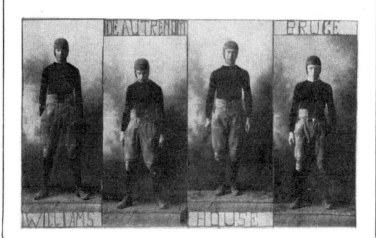

Williams—center—When it comes to passing the "oval" we hand it to Willie. He was T. N. T. on the defensive— Roswell vainly cried, "Somebody stop that center."

DeAutremont—quarterback—a brilliant field general of whom one could always expect the unexpected. Frequently heard on the sidelines—"There he goes,"—Hugh stopped him.

House—full back—Lydia's tackles would always cause his victim to blush. He was one of the fastest men on the field, and a wicked line plunger.

Bruce—left end—Bruce was another light man who made up in nerve what he lacked in size. Our opponents found him to be a hard man to take out. Bob is red-headed. His favorite song is "After the Ball."

Hugh DeAutremont (second from left) as quarterback—"a brilliant field general of whom one could always expect the unexpected." *Bruce Family, Southern Oregon Historical Society, PAM A6, 1923.*

52

barber practice in Oklahoma for $100 and caught a train to Oregon. The two met and continued to Vancouver, where Ray was being held. Judge Holden allowed Roy and Paul to speak before sentencing. Emphasizing that Ray was a good young man who never had been in trouble, they made a strong emotional appeal to the court to release Ray into Roy's custody. Judge Holden was unmoved and sentenced Ray to a full year in the Washington State Reformatory at Monroe.[8]

Following Ray's sentencing, Roy considered alternatives and then made an important decision to stay in Oregon. He wanted to be as close as possible to his jailed twin. Roy was sure that his eyesight was getting worse, so he didn't want to return to barbering if he could avoid it. In Salem, he found a job as an attendant at the Oregon State Mental Hospital, the same facility to which he would be committed twenty-eight years later. But Roy still had to choose which way to go, which mountain to climb. On the one hand, optimistic like his mother and pious, he was inclined to immerse himself in his faith. On the other hand, with the injustice and cruelty he had seen in Ray's treatment, his heart was beginning to harden. He was losing the capacity for forgiveness. He had to choose between God and his twin, and Ray wasn't making the choice easier. When he told Ray that he was considering the priesthood and serving God for life, Ray snapped back that he didn't believe the Bible and thought that the pope was a "rumdum."[9] In the end, Roy felt closer to his brother than to his God.

Ray's choice was easier. He had been surrounded by hardened criminals. He could not get beyond the lifetime of disappointment, resentment and brooding that now controlled his personality. He would find a way to get back at the liars, cheaters and thieves who owed his family for the years of injustice.

In the meantime, younger brother Hugh seemed to be enjoying a much more normal life at home in Lakewood, New Mexico. Twins Ray and Roy were doing what they could to send money home to Belle and keep Hugh and youngest brother Lee in school.

Chapter 3

PLANS

We were sick of life, tired of it all, and we didn't care. So we said we'll play it all on one card. If we win we win and if we lose we lose all.
—Roy DeAutremont, June 1927

FAILED IDEAS

Every venture requires a degree of planning. What weakened the DeAutremonts' planning was their inexperience and lack of critical thinking.

Ray was released from prison in mid-1921. A deeply embittered soul, he lived briefly with Roy, who still worked at the Oregon State Mental Hospital in Salem. They constantly debated religion, the IWW and social injustice. Ray was more persuasive, and Roy's beliefs and attitudes toward the church began to crumble. An ex-con acquaintance arranged a job for Ray, working with him in food service for a Spokane, Washington company. His first day on the job, Ray decided that it wasn't for him, and he returned to Salem. Roy watched Ray grow more morose and possibly suicidal. Seeing what IWW involvement and prison had done to poison Ray, Roy himself grew angry and vengeful.

Ray was not quitting yet; he had an idea. Others he had been in prison with had given him contacts for big-time criminals and gangsters in Chicago.

He planned to get involved with this promising element and score at least one major bank heist. But after he rode the rails to Chicago, none of the contacts developed; he could find no gangsters who wanted to discuss his career alternatives. Also disheartening was his visit to the IWW headquarters in Chicago; he told others that he found it a "miserable, crummy dump."[1] Feeling that they had abandoned him while he served time, he was soured on the Wobblies.

Back from Chicago, Ray found his twin had quit his job at the mental hospital. Ray was surprised by changes in Roy, who had pretty much renounced his faith to pursue a life of crime. Both came to believe that if they could just pull off one big robbery, they could provide for their family forever. At first, Ray objected, but he knew that he could not pull off a daring bank robbery alone. He needed to earn a little operating money, and Roy was the only one who could help with that.

The two went to Portland and got jobs working on a section of a logging road. This was harder work than Roy was used to. They worked and accumulated seventy-five dollars but got fired—the boss told them that they were not putting out the work he needed. A shouting match ensued, and Ray came very close to pulling a pistol from his pocket.

ALONG THE RIGHT-OF-WAY: THE PUTNAMS

From Siskiyou Summit and Tunnel 13's west portal, the railroad extends about eight miles down Cottonwood Creek Canyon, across the California state line and through the mill town of Hilt (also known as Hilts). Terrain and travel always were challenging in these mountains, even with the new Pacific Highway.

Harold Putnam was born in Long Beach, California, in November 1920 to Ross and Alice Putnam. Ross worked as a harbor crane operator, and Alice was a musician who turned down teaching positions because she had a toddler and an infant to care for. Searching for a better place to raise three sons, they headed north toward Oregon in the Model-T "camper" that Ross had engineered. They settled briefly in Gold Hill, Oregon, and Ross began cutting timber for a living. Circumstances not quite ideal, Ross and Alice took out an eighty-acre homestead along Cottonwood Creek and the Southern Pacific over the Siskiyous.

Ned (left) and Harold enjoyed fishing along Cottonwood Creek a few steps from their tent home. *Ross Putnam photo, Putnam family.*

Cottonwood Creek Canyon hardly being an address for a concert pianist, Alice Putnam found it difficult to adjust to primitive living in the Siskiyous. *Ross Putnam photo, Putnam family.*

Life along the Siskiyou line was challenging, especially for Alice. More adventuresome, Ross and their sons did not mind living in a tent while they built their log cabin. The cabin being only a few yards from the track, Harold related years later that his mother never could get used to the trains at all hours of the day and night: those coasting downgrade with brakes and wheels squealing and those pounding and rattling uphill, with several helper engines adding to the noise. Every time a train passed, it felt like an earthquake. Alice was convinced that the next train would cause her little house to fall down around her.

There was constant activity and adventure for the enterprising Putnam males. During much of the time they lived on the homestead, they cut timber for the Avgeris family.[2] Whenever that didn't pay enough to make ends meet, Ross would walk over to Siskiyou Station, look up SP section boss Charlie Prewitt and hire on to do track maintenance for short periods. Harold can remember one especially cold period when his dad spent all night using a steam hose to keep the Siskiyou turntable free of ice so it could turn helper engines.

The railroad was part of everyday life for the Putnams: mail

Still yelling, each side retreated, and a life of crime was postponed for the moment. The twins wandered from one Northwest logging camp to the next, trying to make a few dollars to continue their search for crime opportunities. Part of their problem was physical: at five-feet-six and 135 pounds, they were not built to be lumberjacks or millworkers.

The twins' life of crime would begin (almost) with a bank robbery in the tiny village of Yacolt, Washington, a few short miles from Vancouver and Portland. Ray had made contact with another cellmate, who proposed robbing the local bank over the 1922 Fourth of July weekend. With not many men available for a posse, this could be an easy getaway and a cinch job. When the "associate" failed to meet the twins as planned, they decided to case the opportunity anyway. The first problem they saw was the telephone exchange situated next door to the bank: one robber would be required in the phone office to prevent alarms. Then at least one more was needed to rob the bank (really two) and another to provide a getaway. The twins didn't know how to operate an automobile, so the getaway would require that there be woods nearby for cover and escape. The nearest woods were half a mile away. This clearly was not a foolproof opportunity, so the twins passed it up.

Their next idea, also targeting the holiday weekend, was to rob the bank in Seaside on the northern Oregon coast. Nearly out of funds, the twins "rode the rods" of an Astoria & Columbia River Railroad train from Portland to Seaside. A getaway could be easier that weekend with the traffic and confusion of more "papa trains" operating for the holiday. The A&CR catered to wealthy Portland-area families who summered at the coast and were joined by their businessman husbands and fathers on weekends. Seaside was especially crowded that weekend, and the twins could smell money. They were particularly interested in the bank, but the proximity of the police station was a problem. Just a few doors from the bank, it was too close for comfort. This would not do; in fact, maybe banks in general were a bad idea.

The boys hiked eight or nine miles south over Tillamook Head and along the stretch of sand to the little resort community of Cannon Beach. This, too, was teeming with holiday visitors, and the twins were attracted to a busy confectionery for their "visit." But this also did not feel right to the young would-be crooks. It occurred to them that if they tried

and groceries were dropped off for them at Colestin, Oregon, about three miles down the track from the cabin. SP usually kept a car spotted on the spur at White Point, just west of the tunnel. The Putnams cut firewood and kept the car full for railroaders' kitchens and home heating.[3]

Although train schedules changed, there usually would be a midmorning passenger train laboring upgrade alongside the homestead. With the warm relationship that formed between the Putnam family and railroaders, it became practice on Sundays for the "news butch" or a crewman to throw a copy of the *San Francisco Examiner* to a spot near the cabin. During Christmastime, crews tossed fruit and candy to the Putnams.[1] Also during the holidays, railroaders dropped off Christmas tree orders. Ross and the boys cut and manicured trees and left them near the tunnel for pickup.

Getting to and from school in Ashland could be difficult, especially in bad weather. It was about a mile-and-a-half hike from the homestead cabin to where the Ashland school bus picked up kids at the "Siskiyou Loop" of the Pacific Highway. Overlooking obvious dangers, it seemed much easier to walk *through* the 3,108-foot Tunnel 13 than to trek *across* the brushy mountain above it. Engine crews came to expect kids in the tunnel, and they developed special whistle calls and signals to communicate. Harold remembered those of Engineer Charlie Jones and Fireman Bill Rush. Oftentimes, crewmen allowed the kids to ride through the tunnel in the "crummy" (caboose) or even the locomotive cab. This worked fine except on weekends when there was no school bus waiting at Siskiyou. To play football for Ashland High School, Harold had to run down the mountain to get to the game and then hike back up the hill to get home afterward. Sometimes there'd be a freight to thumb a ride on up the hill.[5]

Living in a primitive mountain cabin was not what Alice had in mind when she left Los Angeles. She made the best of circumstances, and they did improve somewhat. Initially, their homestead cabin had no windows. On their "pack-

a holdup, some foolish hero might resist, inviting a shooting, murder charges and an end to very short careers. The few dollars in the cash register simply weren't worth the risks. Maybe they needed to reconsider targets.

Tired and hungry, they walked back to Seaside and slept the night on the beach. The next day was July 4, and Roy, a runner like his dad, figured that he could win the footrace for badly needed food money. However, the race was not well organized, and Roy was "cheated" out of second-place prize money. Exhausted and starving, the twins rode the rails back to their dad's home in Salem. It seemed like everything they tried pushed them further into desperation.

KNOCKING AROUND

For months, Ray and Roy continued to wander the coast and Willamette Valley, making a few dollars but spending everything in search of crime opportunities. To avoid scrutiny, they changed their names to aliases several times. This was common at the time with little payroll accounting (and if there ever was anyone to hide from). Brothers applying for jobs didn't want an employer to know they were related—if he got mad at one, he probably would fire both.

About the time their father, Paul, moved to Salem, so did older brother Verne, looking for work in the woods or mills. Frugal, Verne worked hard and saved a little money (in contrast to the twins). Paul's new wife, Nellie, had just given birth to Charlie (October 1921), and with Roy helping out at the barbershop, Paul was able to spend time with his young family. However, that didn't last long: Paul was cheated out of his Salem barbershop location. With no others available in Salem, he had to go several miles south to Albany to find a suitable alternative shop.

The boys helped with the move to Albany. A consolation for Roy was that he met and fell in love with an Albany girl, Dorothy Wiberg. Roy and Dorothy seemed to be together constantly. Needing more time at home, Paul asked Roy to take over the Albany shop for a while. He readily agreed. Bitten by the love bug, Roy began thinking family thoughts and forgot about big crime for a while. Smitten briefly by the idea of homesteading on the Oregon coast, he and Ray paid a ten-dollar advance fee to a

ratting" expeditions, they gathered old automobile and irrigation parts. Before long, their cabin had crank-open windows, running water, electricity and auto headlights.[6]

The Putnams lived along the Siskiyou line during the early 1930s, so stories of the DeAutremonts were always part of Putnam family lore—even more so with a chance encounter: during the late 1940s, when the family lived briefly in Brookings on the Oregon coast, a group of student athletes from Southern Oregon Teachers College went to the Oregon coast one summer to play "town team" baseball. Harold, an outstanding high school athlete, was invited to join them. Reciprocating, one dinner guest the Putnams entertained was Charlie DeAutremont (known to most friends as "Chuck"), younger half-brother of Ray, Roy and Hugh DeAutremont. As Harold would say of Chuck, "He was a great athlete and a great guy to know."[7]

In later years, Harold told stories about exploring the DeAutremonts' shelters, which they called Camp #1 and Camp #2 and were located between the Pacific Highway and the railroad track. These were identifiable by the DeAutremonts' confessions and a great number of lead bullets fired into nearby trees at chest height.

GETTING AROUND
THE VALLEY

To clarify how the DeAutremonts and others traveled the Cottonwood Creek Canyon, Harold Putnam offered some local road-building history. After the Pacific Highway was completed through the Siskiyous in 1915, at least one primitive road was carved out of the hillside between the Highway's summit and the Cottonwood Creek area below. Harold's friend Dick Norris lived near the Highway's summit, so the boys used the route almost daily. Harold remembered the road distance between the summit and Tunnel 13 to be about a mile and a half. This was the route the DeAutremonts used between their campsites and to get closer to the tunnel. Years later, during the Great Depression, improving this rough road was a Civilian Conservation Corps (CCC) project, and the route became Mount Ashland Road. Harold remembers foot traffic along the road—tourists renting cottages near the Highway summit hiked it to the homestead to buy goat cheese from the Putnams.[8]

land locator. As it turned out, the agent was crooked, and the swindle prompted Ray to resent society that much more. This experience certainly reminded him of Paul's foolishly buying the New Mexico property sight-unseen years before.

Paul's luck with real estate improving, he found a much better location for a barbershop in a new Eugene building. With the help of the twins, he moved his shop and home to Eugene. The twins continued to help for a while, but then Paul quit the shop and went back into wallpapering and painting. This trade served him well in Colorado, but it wouldn't support the growing number of DeAutremonts in Oregon's Willamette Valley. Ray and Roy moved on, looking for other work.

In late summer or fall of 1922, youngest brother Lee (about fifteen years old) left New Mexico and came to Eugene to spend time with Paul. The visit didn't work out: there was a confrontation and perhaps a belt whipping. Lee decided that he couldn't stay with his dad any longer and contacted Roy for help with room and board.

With little or no work, Ray had grown moody and morose again—"with the blues," as he later described his feelings. That left Roy to manage this pathetic little band of three brothers and their meager resources. Older brother Verne looked them up in Albany.

Although he had saved a few hundred dollars, he couldn't find work now, so he accepted their invitation to room with them for a while. During the weeks around Christmas 1922, the boys moved to lessen their rent, bought clothing, spent time with girlfriends and sought work, hoping to replenish their stash. Their dedication to one another was apparent: although they had little or no money, they shared whatever they had.

Roy grew more worried about Ray's depression. He tried to talk Ray into taking Lee home to New Mexico at Christmastime and then staying for a while to enjoy some of the recreation of their youth: hunting, fishing, riding and old friends. Ray agreed, but he did not leave until spring, around the time Hugh graduated from high school.

The twins discussed their crime plans minimally with family: just a mention to Verne and not at all with Lee or Hugh (at first). Verne was very opposed to anything illegal; he wanted no part of any crime. Over time, the twins considered involving Hugh.

While Ray "repaired" in New Mexico, Roy got jobs for himself and Eddy Wiberg, the fourteen-year-old brother of girlfriend Dorothy, at a camp of the Silver Falls Lumber Company near Silverton, Oregon. When Ray returned, bringing Hugh with him, Roy was able to arrange two more jobs at the same camp. Of course, all four used assumed names.

The twins decided to pitch the idea to Hugh. They explained to him that they had been talking about and planning a high-stakes robbery: a U.S. mail train likely to be carrying a gold shipment and other valuables. The idea of a big heist, one that would put Mom and Dad on "Easy Street" for the rest of their lives, certainly appealed to the three brothers. Newspapers made it clear that a crime wave was on a roll: the popular Roy Gardner was robbing mail trains for hundreds of thousands of dollars. They read somewhere that the Wilson Gang got $3 million and some boys back east $5 million. It seemed too easy. Hugh pondered his career alternatives; he had planned to work one year after high school and then attend college. The best he could imagine after that was working as a clerk in a state bank. It was an easy decision: Hugh was in. This was the beginning of the Siskiyou tragedy.[9] Roy's spirits high now, he considered how he might spend some of his share. He told his brothers, "I could get that girl [Dorothy] and get her all the clothes and nice things that a girl likes to have."[10]

With the twins and Hugh living and working together in Silverton during the spring of 1923, they discussed their great heist constantly. Ray's spirits picked up as he showed an ability to manage details.

1918 NASH

The Pacific Highway offered opportunities, but an automobile was necessary. In Portland, they bought a sporty-looking green 1918 six-cylinder Nash touring car. Now they would have to learn to drive. *Walter Miller.*

There was a big loggers' jamboree at Silverton over the Fourth of July holiday. Loggers had nine days off, and the twins and Hugh went to Portland to buy a used car. At the Burnside Auto Company, they settled on a dandy 1918 Nash touring car for a price of $900 and two months' advance payments ($200). The car came in a green finish instead of standard black. They also bought in Portland camping accessories, an automatic shotgun (using Ray's alias, "William Elliott") and a great deal of ammunition for target practice.

The boys worked at the Silver Falls Lumber Company until just before September 1, when a strike was called. They left on August 28 and used their time off and newly acquired Nash to explore the Pacific Northwest and find the best place to rob a mail train. Because accounts of this time before the holdup do not mention young Eddy Wiberg, he probably went home to Albany after the Silverton jamboree.

Road trips also were opportunities for driving practice; only Hugh had experience operating a motorcar when they bought the Nash. The three ventured out and drove the Pacific Highway as far north as Puget Sound and as far south as Hornbrook, California. With little hesitation, they decided that SP's Siskiyou Summit tunnel, Tunnel 13, offered the best opportunity for a holdup because of its remote site in the mountains, brake test requirement and easy getaway via the Pacific Highway.

Formulating their basic plan, the DeAutremonts would begin their holdup by hiding the Nash twenty-five or thirty miles down the Highway from the tunnel (alongside the railroad track). On the day of the holdup, they would board the locomotive as the train slowed for the brake test at the summit. They would stop the train just before the mail car exited the tunnel and then use persuasion or dynamite to enter the mail car. Inside and with the mail clerk's help, they would identify valuables and fill three knapsacks with loot. Uncoupling the loco and mail car from the rest of the train, they would direct the engineer to race down the track to the hidden auto. Finally, they would transfer the loot to the Nash and use the Pacific Highway to escape their pursuers.

Pilfering a construction cite, the DeAutremont brothers appropriated a Dupont No. 3 plunger-type detonator and blasting accessories. *Smithsonian National Postal Museum.*

If anything went wrong, they would shift to a modified plan, hiding for a while in a "cache" (their term for a hideout stocked with food and supplies) instead of trying to use the auto. They would stop the train, enter and loot the mail car, high-tail it to their cache and wait for things to "cool off" before heading on foot to California.

During one drive about three-quarters of a mile south of SP's Oregon City Station, the boys noticed a construction site of the Rajotte-Winters Corporation, which was installing a siding track for the railroad. Seeing that the work involved blasting, they entered the site and stole a full case of dynamite, blasting caps, wire and a Dupont No. 3 plunger-type detonating machine. They hid these in a locked wooden trunk in the back of the car.

Left: Locals called this abandoned-looking structure sitting atop the tunnel near Toll Road gap "Mount Crest cabin." Much evidence was left behind at this last-days hide out. *Terry Skibby.*

Below: Interior view of Mount Crest cabin. *U.S. Post Office Department.*

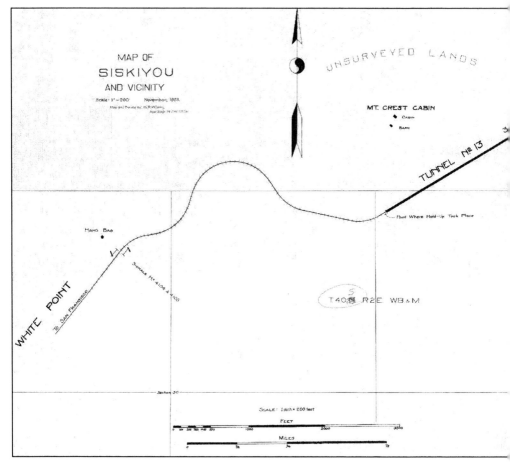

One month after the murders, SP drew an official map of the crime vicinity, including camps, the cache and other crime elements. *Southern Pacific Shasta Division Archives.*

The boys had reason for pessimism: as exciting as this was, robbery of a U.S. mail train was dangerous, especially for novices. Knowing that they could die or fail, the love-struck Roy bought insurance policies worth $60,000. Each had qualms about proceeding, but did not want to appear weak to the other two. Remembering their parents, Roy also named brother Verne a beneficiary. The Guardian Life Insurance Company of Eugene had an excellent reputation for payouts: no questions asked as long as premiums were paid up. While passing through Eugene, the boys bought more supplies from the Love & Love hardware store.

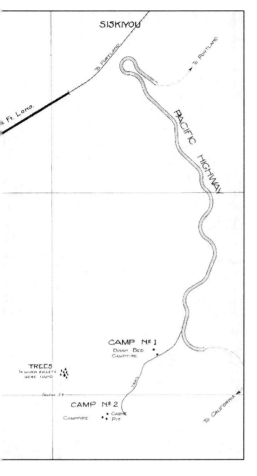

Having selected the tunnel holdup site and a plan, it was time for final details…and then action. The boys got a good area map and compass so they could explore the Cottonwood Creek Valley just beyond Tunnel 13's west portal. They needed to establish a base camp near the tunnel and a more distant hideout cache in case running and hiding would be necessary. This exploration was particularly appealing because they loved outdoor adventure and roughing it. A railroad crew doing track work in the distance gave them some concern, but not enough to scuttle plans.

Driving south on the Pacific Highway about a quarter-mile before its Siskiyou Summit, they found a spot where they could pull off the highway to the west and carefully drive a short distance through the brush. Stopping about three hundred feet from the Highway, they covered the Nash with boughs and brush (the car's green finish helped hide it) and set up a tarpaulin for a tent. This would be their "Camp #1," a site of considerable target practice as the boys began to explore the valley. Nervous about detection, they moved the car a short distance and the tent to "Camp #2." Several days of target practice and tramping the terrain followed.

They found a shack known to locals as the "Mount Crest cabin" and belonging to Seattle businessman Reginald Parsons. Located above the tunnel and a short distance from the old toll road that crossed the Siskiyou ridge, it was positioned well to serve as a base camp. They stocked it with small quantities of food and basic supplies.

An excellent spot for a hideout and cache lay two to three miles west of the tunnel, north of the track and on a north-facing hillside. Located where a tree had fallen across a small creek, leaving shelter beneath, it would be known as the "Brushy Bald Mountain cache." There was not excessive room for three men, but it was big enough and well hidden. The boys stocked the cache with food, bandages, a probe, blood-stopping powder, blankets and extra ammunition. They did not map their explorations well because they thought they could rely on their memories for navigation. They would be sorry that they did not map a route to their cache.

After days of watching trains, the boys selected their target: westbound train No. 13, the San Francisco Express. It almost always arrived on time at Siskiyou. They hadn't heard of a daylight train robbery, but it occurred that daylight, especially in this rough country, could be more help than hindrance. Appealing about train No. 13 was a rumor Ray heard that the train frequently carried gold and cash payrolls. He couldn't recall where he heard that—maybe in a hobo camp coming back from New Mexico.

There was concern about the Nash. At first deemed necessary for the getaway, it had been difficult to drive off the Highway and to camouflage. Although the Pacific Highway greatly improved mountain travel, the Siskiyou country was still too primitive for a fast getaway by automobile. Hugh wanted to take the car to Eugene, where he thought it would be less conspicuous at Paul's house. He would tell Paul that the boys needed to store the car for a few days while reporting to a new job at a logging camp.[11] They could retrieve it later from Eugene for the getaway. The twins weren't keen on the idea but finally agreed. With this decision, the Nash was effectively removed from the plan, and the cache became an inevitability.

Hugh and the Nash bumped and lurched back to the Pacific Highway and headed north for Eugene. Where the Highway approaches Neil Creek near Ashland, he struck a steer said to belong to William High that had wandered onto the pavement. Hugh managed to get the car to the Park Garage in Ashland, but mechanic John McCracken explained that it would take a few days to get necessary parts.

With the car repaired but Hugh unable to communicate with the twins, he got to Eugene as fast as he could. He told Paul his story about having to leave the car and then paid the fare and "rode the cushions" from Eugene back to Ashland. There he planned to hop a train to the summit and find his brothers.

Hugh evidently looked suspicious; a railroad detective stopped and questioned him. Roy had instructed Hugh to mail the insurance receipts to Dorothy, but Hugh lost her address and so still carried the receipts in his pocket. Certainly the nosy detective would have seen and noted Roy's name on the insurance paperwork. He also would have seen the flashlight batteries, bulbs and friction tape that Hugh carried. The detective had a good look at Hugh and a long chat with him. When Hugh lied that he was going to San Francisco, another detective or SP employee "suggested" that he buy a ticket. That pretty much wiped out their money. Trying to avoid boarding the train to San Francisco, Hugh managed to slip away and walked up the mountain to the cache, where the twins awaited.

Hugh was very late in arriving—days later than they had planned. Things suddenly were going wrong: the car accident, the railroad "dick," insurance papers and Hugh having to buy a ticket he wouldn't use. The twins were growing despondent. Roy said later that if Hugh had been just one hour later, there would have been different decisions and no Siskiyou robbery.[12]

The night before Hugh returned, the twins walked down the track a ways for reasons they could not remember. Trying to catch a freight back toward the summit, Roy struck his knee on a platform or post and the pain nearly disabled him. They discussed their despair and considered aborting the holdup. They knew that it would mean not being able to help their mom, dad and brothers. Roy felt he would have to give up his girl. Again fearing the loss of eyesight, he expected to be blind in a year (he never did lose his sight). It seemed pretty clear that Ray's constant melancholia was infecting Roy and Hugh. When Hugh left to take the Nash north, he had about $700. When he returned, he was nearly broke. Conditions seemed hopeless for the brothers.

Worthy of note is debate through the years as to who the DeAutremonts' ringleader was—Ray or young Hugh. The original criminal ideas certainly were Ray's, and he was an effective persuader, but his effectiveness was hindered by bouts of depression. Hugh had more education, more personality and more self-confidence than his brothers. While the twins worried much, Hugh seemed fearless. Reading pulp fiction as he did and idolizing criminals like Jesse James, Hugh was shown to be immature and careless. He did make mistakes.

Chapter 4

THE CRIME

The fella back there says to pull the thing up.
—*Coyl Johnson, October 11, 1923*

SNEAKING DOWN

A little rain fell throughout the night, but October 11, 1923, was a gorgeous morning in the Siskiyous. There was little food left for the DeAutremonts' breakfast, but eating didn't seem important at the time. Days earlier, while planning the holdup, the boys found the seemingly abandoned Mount Crest cabin near a trail that went over the top of Tunnel 13 and through Toll Road Gap. Passing through a notch in the mountain, the trail once was part of the Dollarhide toll road. Litter and trampled grass showed that both the tunnel and path were used regularly by vagrants and SP workers to travel between tunnel portals. The boys felt that the cabin was a safe enough place for making their final holdup plans.

Ray would recall later that the boys spent "one or two" days at the cabin before the holdup—October 10 and maybe the day before.[1] During that time, they had burned Hugh's trunk, its contents and their utensils—anything they would not need that might incriminate them later.

The tiny railroad hamlet of Siskiyou was a good spot for a train robbery. *Southern Oregon Historical Society, #14773.*

Earlier photos show the footpath (far right) between the tunnel portals. The east portal is pictured. *Southern Oregon Historical Society, #11187.*

The boys were pessimistic. Things had gone wrong for several days, so they began to think that their caper might fail. But feeling that they had nothing to lose in this life, they decided to proceed. With plans finalized, they set out to rob train No. 13, the San Francisco Express. They soaked their shoes in creosote and sprinkled black pepper around the cabin to put off any tracking dogs. They dressed in overalls and covered their faces with grease paint to look like SP "gandy dancers" (track workers). They took three packsacks to the tunnel to carry the loot. In case someone might spot them, they concealed the detonator in another pair of coveralls. Carrying just the equipment they'd need, the three walked to the west portal of the tunnel. The detonator was unwrapped and placed just outside the tunnel on the north side of the track. They uncoiled the wire from a point inside the tunnel to the detonator outside. Using brush, they made a half-hearted effort to hide the dynamite, caps, wire and detonator.

The boys had collected weapons whenever opportunity permitted. On this morning, Ray carried an automatic twelve-gauge shotgun, and each of the three had a .45-caliber pistol tucked into his belt.

The DeAutremonts had observed the train's routine for several days. It almost always arrived at Siskiyou on time at 12:35 p.m. Timing would be critical this day; the boys could not be even seconds late. With dynamite and accessories in place, Roy and Hugh started their hike over the hill. Ray stayed behind at the west portal. Carrying the twelve-gauge, he tried to relax but couldn't stop pacing as he chain-smoked and awaited the train. With dry brush and dynamite nearby, smoking was not a good idea. It is not known whether he heard the moaning of pine trees swaying in a slight breeze or Cottonwood Creek babbling not far away. There was the pungent scent of last night's rain on the sagebrush. If Ray noticed any of these, he could think only about the holdup routine they had gone over so many times.

The breeze was westerly, so Ray didn't hear the train right away. There it was: three short whistles ("stop at the station"). He heard the loud *clank* as the brakeman uncoupled the helper engine.

Down at the track, the helper was cut off and quickly switched aside; now No. 3626 was on the point, and Bates was the engineer in charge. One well-dressed passenger walked forward; he studied the engine as though he wanted to talk trains with the engineer.[2] With a polite smile, Bates shook his head to signal that he was too busy to chat. He heard someone beckon the man back to the train, addressing him as "Doctor." The enthusiast smiled back at Sid, nodded understanding and turned to go back to his car. Two long whistle blasts rang out ("releasing brakes and proceeding"). The station

A gandy dancer crew like this one rushed to the tunnel and arrived just after the DeAutremonts took off running. *Elhart Collection, Box 9 #42D, Southern Oregon Historical Society.*

Busy summit: the crew of a westbound freight ignores a helper on the turntable as the freight plunges into Tunnel 13. *Elhart Collection, Southern Oregon Historical Society Box 8, #35.*

agent hurried along the narrow platform to meet and give train orders to Conductor Marrett.

There was more activity at Siskiyou Station than Roy expected. A long whistle followed two shorts ("second section following"). There were many workers: laborers and men carrying map cases and surveying equipment. Near the east end of the Toll Road Gap, where the trail meets the rail yard, Roy and Hugh cautiously walked the last few yards down the hillside to the braking power track. Roy was nervous; he kept looking around to see if anyone was paying attention to them. Later, he would claim (almost brag) that no one observed or seemed suspicious of the two. He was wrong. Discussions later would suggest that at least six SP surveyors and laborers noticed a couple of dark-skinned, strange-acting characters crouching and running behind the string of old cars parked on the braking power track. Some saw the duo walk toward the engine as Bates began to accelerate for his brake test, but they disappeared quickly. During Hugh DeAutremont's trial in June 1927, Special Prosecutor George Neuner questioned SP survey rodman Ray Finneran regarding the shady characters he claimed to have seen:

> *GN: What did you observe at that point?*
> *RF: Two men.*
> *GN: Where were these two men?*
> *RF: Right next to the braking power track right alongside the cars there.*
> *GN: How did these men act to attract your attention?*
> *RF: The way they were sneaking down around the cars there.*
> *GN: What do you mean by sneaking down?*
> *RF: They would go down about a car length and get in between the cars and then another car length and get in between the cars…There were seven or eight cars on that track and they were going from one car to another, sneaking down as they came to the couplers.*
> *GN: Did you get a clear view of these men?*
> *RF: I did.*[3]

Roy was more experienced riding the rails than young Hugh; he motioned Hugh to board first. He was concerned that the train was accelerating faster than he had expected—maybe ten to twelve miles per hour instead of the customary five or six during the brake test. Hugh reached out and easily grasped a tender "grab iron" (ladder wrung) in the "blind sill" (space between the tender and mail car). He turned to Roy and saw that he was

As soon as it could be located and transported, a ceiling scaffold was moved to Tunnel 13's west portal. Thorough repairs would require heavy maintenance. *Terry Skibby.*

falling behind. Hugh quickly extended a leg. Roy frantically grabbed Hugh's foot and strained to pull himself aboard. He felt pain in the knee he had injured in the dark a few nights before.

As Roy struggled to board, his .45-caliber pistol slipped out of his belt and fell to the roadbed below. It banged loudly and danced on the track as the train passed over it. For a split second, they both feared that the weapon might discharge, but it did not. The boys crawled onto the top of the tender, gained their footing and gathered their wits. Roy's only weapon now was a blackjack. It was said later that Bates, seeing the two invaders, pulled his throttle wide open, hoping to toss off the freeloaders. That is not likely, as Bates certainly understood that steam engines do not respond quickly to control changes.

Roy took charge:

> *I told Hugh to give the engineer his orders and I would give the fireman his. The orders we gave were these: "Stop your train with the engine cab just clear of the tunnel. If you fail to do so the fireman will take your place*

A car parked at White Point siding showing mail end damage. Popped rivet lines and peeled steel panels attest to the force of the blast. *Terry Skibby.*

The next day, officials inspected the car. *U.S. Post Office Department.*

because you will be dead." And I gave the fireman his instructions: "If the engineer fails to stop the train with the cab just clear of the tunnel you are to take his place because he will be dead." They agreed to it. I told him to keep his eyes off of me, that he couldn't do that. The engineer acted like he thought it was a joke. He didn't act like he thought it was anything very serious. He could see we were young, just kids, but he carried out our instructions to the letter.[1]

Mexican tunnel maintainers working near the east portal seemed to ignore the engine, even as they paused to let the train pass.

Ray crouched outside the west portal. He watched the iron monster approach him and wondered if it really would stop. It did, with just the engine cab protruding from the tunnel. Just inside was the first car, the mail car. Hugh ordered Engineer Bates and Fireman Seng to climb down from the right side of the cab (engineer's side). Hugh followed and marched them a few yards to a spot near the detonator. Ray heard the mail car door roll open and saw the mail clerk, Elvyn Dougherty, stick out his head.

Like others on the train, Dougherty wondered why it stopped. Many aboard knew that a brake test was required, but it did not call for a complete stop. When Dougherty moved to close the door, Ray raised his shotgun and fired. Shot ricocheted off the door and side of the car. Ray did not hit Dougherty, and the clerk slammed and locked the door.

A subject of debate has been whether or not the DeAutremonts intended to hurt the mail clerk—or anyone. Roy later explained that the plan was to shoot open the mail car door and scare the clerk into cooperating. They would use dynamite only if they couldn't get the door open. Figuring that it would take a posse about forty-five minutes to reach the site, the robbers would have to work fast. They didn't intend to kill the clerk right away because they needed him. But there could be no question about the boys' intent to kill and their disregard for human life: "[We] did not want to kill him, because we wanted that man to find the valuable mail for us so as not to lose any valuable time, wanted that man to fork over the valuable mail… We would have killed him before we left in order that there would be no eye witnesses. That was also the plan as to the engineer and fireman." Cleary, dead men tell no tales.[5]

Dougherty, in the postal compartment, was not alone onboard the mail car. Express messenger helper Hugh Haffey was in the express compartment, deadheading from Ashland to Hornbrook. Suddenly, Haffey heard an unusual noise, like two sharp cracks, and thought, as did others, that the

		62'-11⅝"		63'-0"		63'-0"		63'-0"	
		60'-1½"		60'-1½"		60'-1⅛"		60'-1½"	
To Roseburg		MAIL	BAGGAGE	BAGGAGE		BAGGAGE		BAGGAGE	
	ENGINE	N° 3626	O.&.C.	N° 5037	S.P. N° 6327		S.P. N° 6430		S.P. N° 6421
36'-0	55'-6	118'-5⅝" To Portal		181'-5⅝" To Portal		244'-5⅝" To Portal		307'-5⅝" To Portal	

On the morning of October 11, 1923, SP Train 1-13 ran heavy with a consist of eight cars. A second section followed. *Southern Pacific Shasta Division Archives.*

In a re-created scene, the big Deck emerges from the west portal, site of the holdup. *U.S. Post Office Department.*

78

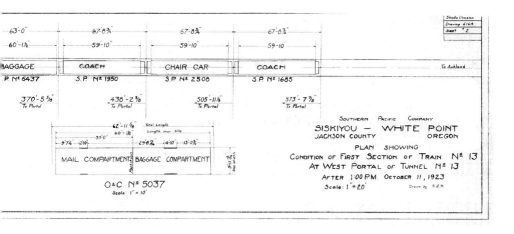

engineer or fireman had dropped tools. But when Haffey slid open the door on the right side and looked toward the tunnel opening, he saw what must have curdled his blood: two figures running around the tunnel entrance and a third backed up to the right side of the engine with his hands high in the air. As his eyes adjusted, Haffey saw that the two were dressed in dark clothing and wore hats—one like a sombrero or maybe a Stetson. He quickly ducked back into the car, closed the door and ran back toward the next car to warn messengers that the train was being held up. He didn't get far.

Ray understood quickly that Dougherty would not cooperate, so it was time for the dynamite. Roy grabbed the loose wires and climbed up into the blind sill. Ray hoisted up to him the heavy grip filled with dynamite. Roy placed the grip on the sill, inserted the wires into blasting caps and climbed down. Later making the excuse that he was not experienced with dynamite, Roy used not a few sticks but *all* the dynamite.

This was not the routine they had rehearsed, and Ray should have known better. Ray should have watched Roy place the dynamite, but he was distracted by the mail clerk slamming the door. The boys were agitated by the constant ringing of the loco's bell. Roy muttered and cursed "that damned bell!" Their plan called for Ray to detonate the dynamite if it became necessary, but as they ran out of the tunnel, Roy got to the Dupont first. He threw himself onto the plunger, and a terrific explosion shook the mountain, filling the tunnel with dust and smoke. Ray was in shock, disbelief.[6] As Haffey ran into the next car, the blast knocked him to the floor and he lay unconscious for several minutes.

NO TURNING BACK

Startled employees in the train and around Siskiyou Station thought that the loco's boiler had blown up. The agent ran into the tiny station building and banged out a quick telegraphic message to the nearest stations (Hilt, Hornbrook and Ashland): "Boiler explosion in tunnel, no details."

Terrified passengers could not imagine what forces had caused train lights to go out and car windows to shatter. Concerns quickly turned to escape. As rumors of a boiler explosion spread, some considered walking back out of the tunnel to Siskiyou. However, that required a half-mile trek through the dark and unknown, nearly impossible for frightened children and ladies in travel attire. Everyone could smell the smoke and gases, but no one knew exactly what conditions were in the tunnel. Most decided to stay onboard the stalled train and await help.

Roy saw that his carelessness was causing the holdup to unravel. First he lost his pistol, and then he destroyed the mail car by using far too much dynamite. The plan called for uncoupling the loco and mail car from the rest of the train and then speeding down the track while pillaging its valuables.[7] Was that still possible? Hugh directed Bates back to his place in the cab. Knowing that he was in trouble with his brothers, Roy went back into the tunnel to uncouple the loco and mail car from the rest of the train. He borrowed Ray's .45, having lost his own. That left Ray with the shotgun. Roy took Seng with him, but the big fireman was overcome by smoke and gases before he could be of any use. Roy told him to leave the tunnel and go stand beside the loco with his hands in the air.

Roy's flashlight was inadequate; he could not see into the mail car or more than a few inches in front of him. Getting down on hands and knees, he could just make out a large hole in the mail car's floor and a pile of debris on the track below it. Partially burned pieces of mail were everywhere. What he definitely could not see anywhere in the mail car were transfer boxes of gold. These heavy wooden cases—usually thirty-six inches long, eighteen inches wide and six inches high—would have been easy to spot had they been onboard.[8]

Heavy damage and smoke kept Roy from climbing into the car. Their only hope for salvaging valuables required getting the mail car out of the tunnel. Shaking his flashlight as though that would make it shine brighter, Roy strained his eyes, trying to determine if the couplers were damaged. Just then, he made out a human form walking toward him from the rear of

One had to enter the car to appreciate the carnage. *Terry Skibby.*

More examination of the heavily damaged car—looking for clues. *Southern Oregon Historical Society, #6791.*

the train, guided by the red fusee (emergency flare) he held. Roy assumed correctly that this was a railroader—deadheading brakeman "Coyl" Johnson. The next day would be Johnson's thirty-seventh birthday.[9]

A few minutes earlier, Johnson and a few others, led by Conductor Marrett, were sure that there had been a boiler explosion and were anxious to work their way forward to help the enginemen. The terrific roar of steam escaping broken lines was almost deafening. The group didn't get far. Some were overcome by smoke and fumes, and Marrett wanted to go back to find enclosed flashlights, fearing that open-flame fusees might trigger another explosion. With Marrett's encouragement, they decided to retreat back toward the end of the train and regroup—all except Johnson, who announced that he would try to continue forward.

Approaching the mail car on the left side of the train, Johnson was challenged by Roy. "Stop right there!" Roy leveled the .45 he'd borrowed from Ray. A surprised Johnson asked, "Who are you?"

"None of your business," Roy fired back menacingly.[10]

Johnson saw clearly that he was in the middle of a train robbery. He also could see tremendous damage to the steel-sheet mail car through breaks

Damaged mail car O&C 5037 is moved to Sacramento for a complete rebuild. *Robert Church.*

OREGON STATE BOARD OF HEALTH
CERTIFICATE OF DEATH

State Registered No. **197**

1 PLACE OF DEATH

County **Jackson** ... State **Oregon** Local Registered No. **66**

Township ... or Village ... or

City **Siskiyou Station** No. ... St. ... Ward
(If death occurred in a hospital or institution, give its name instead of street and number)

2 FULL NAME Sidney Lloyd Bates

(a) Residence. No. ... St., **Dunsmuir, Calif.**
(Usual place of abode) (If nonresident, give city or town and state)
Length of residence in city or town where death occurred yrs. mos. ds. How long in U. S., if of foreign birth? yrs. mos. ds.

PERSONAL AND STATISTICAL PARTICULARS

3 SEX **Male**	4 COLOR OR RACE **White**	5 Single, Married, Widowed or Divorced (write the word) **Married**

5a If married, widowed, or divorced
HUSBAND of
(or) WIFE of

6 DATE OF BIRTH (month, day, and year) **Dec. 30, 1871**

7 AGE	Years	Months	Days	If less than 1 day ...hrs. or ...min.
	51	**9**	**11**	

8 OCCUPATION OF DECEASED
(a) Trade, profession, or particular kind of work **Engineer**
(b) General nature of industry, business, or establishment in which employed (or employer)
(c) Name of employer **S.P.Co.**

9 BIRTHPLACE (city or town) **Norwalk**
(State or country) **Ohio**

10 NAME OF FATHER

11 BIRTHPLACE OF FATHER (city or town)
(State or country)

12 MAIDEN NAME OF MOTHER

13 BIRTHPLACE OF MOTHER (city or town)
(State or country)

14 Informant **Mrs. William ...**
(Address) **Dunsmuir, Calif.**

15 Filed **Oct 12, 1923** *F.J. Swedenborg* (M.D.)
Registrar

CORONER'S CERTIFICATE OF DEATH

16 DATE OF DEATH (month, day, and year) **Oct. 11, 1923**

17 I HEREBY CERTIFY, That I took charge of the remains described above, held an **Inquest** thereon
(Inquest, Autopsy or Inquiry)
and from the evidence obtained by said **Inquest**
(Inquest, Autopsy or Inquiry)
find that said deceased came to **his** death on the day stated above.

The CAUSE OF DEATH * was as follows:

Gun shot wounds inflicted by unknown parties. "Murder"
(duration) yrs. mos. days.

CONTRIBUTORY
(Secondary)
(duration) yrs. mos. days.

18 (Signed) **W. W. P. Hy...** M. D.
(Examining physician)
John Mc...
(Coroner)
Oct. 13, 23 (Address) **Medford, Or**

* State the Disease Causing Death, or in deaths from Violent Causes, state (1) Means and Nature of Injury, and (2) whether Accidental, Suicidal, or Homicidal. (See reverse side for additional space.)

19 PLACE OF BURIAL, CREMATION OR REMOVAL **Dunsmuir, Calif.** | DATE OF BURIAL **Oct. 15, 1923**

20 UNDERTAKER **J.P.Dodge & Sons** | ADDRESS **Ashland, Ore**

Exact statement of OCCUPATION is very important. See Instructions on back of certificate. Or DEATH in plain terms, so that it may be properly classified. (left margin)

Death certificate of Engineer Sidney Bates. *State of Oregon Center for Health Statistics.*

in the smoke. In several places, rivets had popped, and seams had broken. There was no sign of Dougherty. Roy convinced Johnson that his life had never been in greater danger than right then and that he'd have to cooperate if he wanted to live. He told Johnson to uncouple the train from the mail car—they needed to get the car out of the tunnel quickly.

After cursory examination, Johnson explained that the couplers on the loco tender end of the mail car and possibly the other end were damaged. To uncouple, the loco would have to inch forward while the cut lever was lifted. Roy didn't know if he could trust the trainman, but he had few choices. Roy yelled, "Go out there and tell the fellas to have the engineer pull it forward." Then Roy warned, "Just keep your hands high in the air!"[11]

Johnson walked forward alongside the train. The fusee was hard to hold over his head. Without thinking, he lowered his arms as he walked out into the daylight and fresh air. Ray and Hugh were nearby, debating what to do next. They either heard Johnson's footsteps as he walked the ballasted roadbed or caught a glimpse of him from the corner of an eye. Wheeling around on this stranger, they figured he was someone who had just killed their brother Roy in the tunnel. Without hesitation, they

WHO SHOT COYL?

Seeing Johnson on his knees and in great pain, either Ray or Hugh fired again at Johnson (Hugh, according to Ray later). Who fired that third shot? Not Roy—he was in the tunnel waiting for the train to move so he could uncouple it. Hugh's account later does not mention the third shot. The autopsy following the crime was clumsy, so Johnson's body was exhumed and reexamined just before the trial. The wounds were consistent with one shotgun blast and a single .45 pistol shot. A second shotgun blast would have been obvious but was not evident. Most likely, Hugh fired his pistol twice, missing the first time because Johnson was then several yards away from Hugh. Because Johnson was still alive when rescuers arrived, it is not likely that he was shot three times (i.e., twice by Hugh).[12]

both fired their weapons, Ray a shotgun blast to the abdomen and Hugh his .45. Johnson went down on his knees but was still able to speak, saying, "Those fellows back there want you to pull the thing up."[13]

When the train did not move forward, Roy ran out of the tunnel to find out what the delay was. Shocked to see Johnson crumpled on the ground, he yelled at Ray and Hugh, "Didn't he tell you to move the engine?!" At this point, it seemed that the brothers had killed two men (Mail Clerk Dougherty and Johnson) but could not even get into the smoking mail car. Leaving Fireman Seng standing beside the engine, Hugh ordered Bates back into the cab and told him to move the locomotive. The ten big drive wheels did not turn. Bates protested, "I can't move it; the wheels must be on the ground!"

Hugh remained in the cab with Bates, and Roy went back to the tunnel, waiting for the engine to move so he could lift the cut lever. Ray ran around the engine, tender and mail car looking for whatever was preventing the engine from moving. If there was a mechanical problem, it wasn't obvious to the boys. Most likely the explosion broke the train line (air brakes), causing the brakes to "dynamite" (suddenly lose all air pressure so they apply fully). This could not have been remedied without maintenance.[11]

HEROICS?

In different accounts of the crime later, Engineer Bates generally was portrayed as a quiet, compliant little man. In fact, this may not describe him accurately. In later conversation, Hugh spoke suspiciously of Bates trying to thwart their robbery: "If you and the world must know—Yes, d--- them, we killed them. I shot the engineer! He wouldn't turn a wheel for me, the d--- double-crosser! And he told me he was trying to move that train!"[15]

Bates's train was being hijacked and he and Conductor Marrett were responsible for passengers' safety. Wild-eyed youngsters were running around waving weapons, and probably two men—Dougherty and Johnson—were dead. Bates did not have time or resources; he needed a miracle to gain control of the situation but he didn't have it. Bandits held a gun to his head, yelling for him to move the train. Twice he insisted that the train would not move, and that was certainly possible. In the dark, it was difficult to see damage: locked brakes, damaged couplers, derailed wheels, explosion debris and tunnel wall clearance. But there was some indication that the loco *could* move, so it is possible that Bates could have cooperated with the bandits and pulled the train out of the tunnel had he wanted to.

Death certificate of Elvyn Dougherty. *State of Oregon Center for Health Statistics.*

Conductor Marrett was the first trainman to reach the locomotive cab who would live to tell about it (Johnson had been shot a few minutes earlier). With knowledge of steam locomotive operation, Marrett later explained how he found valves and pumps shut off in the cab. He recited intentional actions required to place the engine into the configuration he found: "Well there would be four operations that were necessary. The first operation would be closing the throttle, the steam valve, and then it would take a separate operation to close the tank valve, it would take a separate operation to close the pump throttle and it would also take a separate operation to shut the air brake valve."[16]

With the chaos of the situation, it was possible that Bates closed valves and disabled the loco without anyone noticing. The enginemen realized that the robbers planned to take the burning car down the track to pillage it. It was too late to prevent loss of life, but if the loco and mail car were

Death certificate of Charles "Coyl" Johnson. *State of Oregon Center for Health Statistics.*

stuck in the tunnel, maybe these young robbers would run away without killing anyone else.

SP No. 3626's bell had been sounding for several minutes, and Roy's agitation was worsening. Clearly, the plan wasn't working; maybe it was time for the boys to eliminate witnesses and run for the hideout. Fireman Seng still stood on the ground near Roy, his hands in the air. Roy looked at Seng and then asked Ray, "What about him?" Ray answered, "We don't need him." Roy placed his .45 to Seng's temple and pulled the trigger once. The husky fireman slumped to the roadbed.

There were few choices to make now with things happening so quickly. Bates stood quietly looking out the window on the left side of the cab deck, Fireman Seng's position. Standing next to the engineer, Hugh raised his .45 to Bates's right ear and fired one shot.[17]

CARNAGE AND CHAOS

Because this crime involved many people and simultaneous actions, understanding it requires looking at it several times from different perspectives.

Onboard 1-13, trainmen conducted the brake test between the station and the tunnel. The test didn't require a full stop, but when it occurred, no one was particularly concerned. Railroaders onboard figured that trainmen were making minor adjustments to the brakes and that they would be back underway momentarily.

Conductor Marrett walked to the front of the first coach (SP1950), where conductors used a small desk as their office. Marrett planned to catch up on his ticket report. Because he expected to spend only a few minutes in the tunnel, he left his light unlit. He waited as patiently as a conductor can wait. After several minutes, he stood up—just as a "tremendous concussion" shook the train. The window beside him shook and broke, cutting him on his face and hands. He was sure that the loco boiler had blown up.

Thinking of the souls onboard, he walked through the three passenger cars, talking to and trying to comfort folks any way he could. With fumes and smoke filling the tunnel and swirling in through broken windows, passengers were on the verge of panic. Marrett assured them there was nothing to worry about and that remaining calm was in their best interest. They seemed to accept that. Passengers quieted, and Marrett prepared to go forward to the loco to help the enginemen. He walked through the cars and got to the cabinets where fusees were stored for signaling and emergencies. He grabbed several and then went to the vestibule to exit the car.

Five other railroaders appeared and joined Marrett on the right side of the train for the trek forward: SP civil engineer Herbert C. Micander, Head Brakeman Lowell Grim, deadheading conductors Samuel L. Clayton of Dunsmuir and George C. Stevens of Ashland and deadheading brakeman Coyl Johnson of Ashland.[18]

Conditions in the tunnel were getting worse. Everything was black; smoke obscured daylight at the portal. Fumes made it nearly impossible to breathe, and Marrett feared that with the buildup of gases, the open-flame fusees might trigger another explosion. The would-be rescuers got as far as the smoldering mail car. The force of the blast a few minutes earlier seemed to have thrown the car toward the right tunnel wall, blocking them from continuing along that side of the tunnel. They turned around and went

Death certificate of Marvin Seng. *State of Oregon Center for Health Statistics.*

back—all except Johnson, who said that he planned to cross under a car and continue forward. This was the last time they'd see Coyl alive.

With the explosion, three other would-be rescuers sprang into action. Leonard and Chester Smith and another member of the tunnel maintenance gang were eating lunch near the east tunnel portal when the blast occurred. Suspecting a boiler explosion, they grabbed fire extinguishers and hiked over the tunnel to its west end. The trip required about twenty minutes and their arms grew tired from carrying the heavy extinguishers. Reaching the west tunnel portal, the workers found Bates, Seng and Johnson dead or dying, and there was no sign of Dougherty. Seeing no fire at the time, they started to climb into the damaged end of the mail car. Suddenly, it occurred to them that this could be a holdup. They decided to get out of there and return to Siskiyou Station to report what they found. They returned as they had

Forms 30

C. S.
1-23-110,000—2

(OWNER) Oregon & California Railroad COMPANY,

(OPERATED BY) Southern Pacific COMPANY. GENERAL MANAGER'S

Shasta DIVISION. NO.

Office of J. W. FitzGerald, Supt.

Dunsmuir, Cal., Feb. 5 192 4

(Place)   (Date)

AUTHORITY FOR EXPENDITURE.

of $ 15,816.00 is requested for the purpose

of   to the property as follows:

Station Location: Siskiyou, Oregon

Mile Post No. 412.2

Description of project:

General Supt's M. P. No.

Division Supt's A.G.M. No. 3878

Supt's of M. P. No.

No.

Valuation Section O. & C. R.R.

No. 1 Oregon

(State)

Reference to companion

Forms 30

Fire Protection for Tunnel #13.

Recommendations:

Detailed Estimate Attached.

Tunnel #13 on the Siskiyou Mountains is 3108 feet
in length, and is timber lined throughout. The topography
at this point is such that in case of a fire in the tunnel
a serious tie up of main line traffic would occur, as it is
impossible to build a temporary line around.

Propose to install a fire protection system for
this tunnel which will consist of suitable storage supply
at each end, connected by a 3 inch fire line with 1½ inch
hydrants at intervals throughout.

If fire in the tunnel should be discovered in a
reasonable length of time after starting, with facilities
provided in this estimate, the chances of extinguishing
would be good.

No fire protection except water barrels and fire
extinguishers are provided at this tunnel now.

Authority for this appropriation is requested.

Prints Attached A.G.M. 3878.

B. Ballard

GENERAL FIRE INSPECTOR

SUMMARY OF ESTIMATE				Submitted by
INVESTMENT ACCOUNT NOS.	DEBIT	LEDGER VALUE PROPERTY RETIRED	NET CHANGE OR CREDIT TO INVESTMENT ACCOUNTS	(Title)
				Recommended by (Title)
5	15816.		15816.	3878 (Title)
TOTAL CAPITAL ACCOUNT				(Title)
Operating Expenses				

SP considers a fire protection system for Tunnel 13—after the fact. *Southern Pacific Shasta Division Archives.*

come: over the tunnel. Had they traveled through the tunnel, they would have bumped into Marrett, with flashlights now, making another attempt to reach the locomotive.[19]

Having retreated to the rear of the train just a few minutes earlier, Conductor Marrett found flashlights and asked for volunteers to return with him to help the enginemen. Young Lawrence E.C. Joers volunteered. Joers was a graduate of Walla Walla College in Washington State and trained as a nurse. In future years, he would attend Loma Linda Medical School and become a physician, but on this date, he was a nurse, not a doctor.[20]

Crouching low to breathe, Marrett and Joers reached the smoldering mail car. The tunnel was narrow and completely dark—some kind of damage blocked their advance on the right side. They ducked down low near the mail car's rear truck (rear wheel set) and crawled under the car to the left side of the track. With more room on the left side, they were able to continue forward to the loco. Marrett climbed the gangway in search of the crew, while Joers continued forward and around the front of the loco. Marrett found his old friend Sid Bates sprawled on the left (fireman's) side of the cab floor. He lay half on his back and half on his side, his head pointing forward toward the boiler. Marrett noticed a little blood oozing from Sid's mouth and ear; he was sure that the concussion of a boiler explosion had taken Bates's life, yet the boiler appeared to be intact.

Not seeing Fireman Seng, Marrett crossed to the engineer's side of the cab and looked out the gangway. Beneath him and just a few feet from the track was Seng, apparently lifeless in a crumpled position next to a portal bent (a simple wooden support). A few feet beyond was Coyl Johnson, in a stooped or crouched position, his feet sticking out from under him. Marrett assessed correctly that he could do nothing for Seng but thought that perhaps Johnson was still alive.

Just then, SP civil engineer Micander returned from the rear of the train and hurried to where he saw Marrett trying to help Johnson. The two figured that, with conditions as bad as they witnessed in the tunnel, this brakeman had been overcome by smoke and gases. They began pumping Johnson's arms to administer artificial respiration.[21] Joers was a few steps behind Marrett and eager to save lives. After cursory examinations of Bates and Seng, Joers caught up with the others trying to help Johnson.

Surprised to find blood on his hands, Joers told the others that Johnson was wounded. "No," they disagreed; the blood must have come from Fireman Seng falling out of the cab. Johnson was gasping, so they were sure that he had been gassed in the tunnel. This did not seem right to Joers. Johnson

Above: Workers begin repairing track. Three or more enter the tunnel at the west portal. *John Palmer photo, Arthur Perry Collection, Southern Oregon Historical Society.*

Opposite, top: Track workers begin arriving from nearby White Point and place blankets over the murdered trainmen. *John Palmer photo, Arthur Perry Collection, Southern Oregon Historical Society.*

Opposite, bottom: The copyright symbols suggest that John B. Palmer was probably the first photographer to reach the crime scene. *John Palmer photo, Arthur Perry Collection, Southern Oregon Historical Society.*

was still alive but in horrible pain. Joers decided to cut and remove clothing to look for injuries. Doing so, they observed in the brakeman's chest and abdomen nine wounds appearing to be from buckshot fired at point-blank range. One small hole could have come from a pistol. They tried to make Johnson more comfortable, but he died in their arms.

Having medical help now (too late as it was), they returned to Seng's body. Joers determined that the fireman had been shot through the temples. At first, they thought that there had been a second shot because there also was an arm wound. However, that would turn out to be from the same shot that caused the head wound because Seng was standing with arms raised when he was shot. Moving to Bates, Joers was deeply saddened by this, their second meeting today. Bates had been shot twice—once in the ear, the bullet exiting the other, and again through the jaw, evidently as he fell.

93

Along the track, loose boards covered shallow ditches that drained groundwater from the tunnel. Marrett, Micander and Joers used several to construct makeshift stretchers. They removed Bates, Seng and Johnson to the hillside area a few feet north of the tracks. The deceased would remain there for several hours while lawmen and investigators traveled to the scene. With all the excitement and confusion of the crime, security was poor, and there was little cooperation between agencies.

Ironically, the first to leave the chaotic murder scene was the one missing victim: Elvyn Dougherty. Loco No. 3626 and the devastated mail car, with the remains of the mail clerk evidently still aboard, were pulled down to White Point siding just after the train was pulled from the opposite (east) end of the tunnel. Between White Point and the tunnel was an SP telephone. Marrett used it twice—once to report an apparent boiler explosion and again to correct that to a holdup and shooting.

LEAVING THE TUNNEL

After the discovery of the three grisly murders, the mail clerk was still missing. Equipped with flashlights now, Conductor Marrett asked Joers and American Railway Express Company express messengers helper Henry B. Carter (of Ashland) to enter the mail car and look for Dougherty. There was no fire at the moment; Carter and Joers agreed and crawled into the car. The partition was down, and there were mail sacks scattered everywhere. Their flashlights helped, but they found no sign of Dougherty.

Then Joers, trudging through the debris, stepped on something soft. Moving to get off of it, something else seemed to slap him in the face. Directing his flashlight upward, he recognized human flesh and intestines hanging from the car's frame. Shining his light down toward the floor, he discovered the partial torso of a man—head, chest and arms.

Surrounded by debris and embers, the body was disfigured and dismembered. The only clothing was a piece of shirt collar around the neck. They carefully turned the body to identify it. From having worked with him on other trains, Carter recognized Dougherty. Joers and Carter wasted no time leaving the car.[22]

One of the first trainmen to swing into action when 1-13 mysteriously stopped in the tunnel was Rear Brakeman James Benjamin. Charged with protecting the rear of his train from collision, he had to flag it (light and place a red fusee on the track in the tunnel or place flags along the track outside in the sunlight). At this point, it didn't matter why the train stopped—just that it was blocking the tunnel. This was critical, because train 2-13 was known to be just a few minutes from Siskiyou Station. There could be no wasting time.

Suddenly, a terrific force like a giant hand seemed to scoop up Benjamin and propel him out of the tunnel. Outside and flagging again, he found a Colt .45-caliber pistol lying on the track. Picking it up, he found it loaded and cocked, with the safety off. He was far more concerned about the approaching second section—Benjamin gave the weapon to another SP brakeman milling in the gathering crowd.[23] It was eventually turned over to the Jackson County sheriff.

In those first few minutes after the horrific explosion, confusion became chaos; there were souls on the train who were struggling to breathe. Before the explosion, deadheading conductors Samuel Clayton and George Stevens were seated in the chair car just across the aisle from deadheading brakeman Johnson. No one had been very concerned about the train stopping, but the blast changed everything. Windows rattled and broke. Stevens reported that most of the lights in the chair car went out.

Instinctively, Stevens and Clayton jumped up to help Marrett calm terrified passengers. Many had been cut by window glass. Having done what they could to restore order, the two alighted the train and joined Marrett, Grim, Johnson and Micander to go forward and deal as best they could with a boiler explosion. Marrett found flashlights to replace fusees, but he lost most of his original rescue team in the chaos. Micander and Grim struck out on their own to help others. Johnson had continued forward to the engine, and now Stevens and Clayton decided to get the stalled train out of the tunnel.

Stevens remained with the train, while Clayton sprinted out of the tunnel and back to the station at Siskiyou. He needed a locomotive; 1-13's helper was sitting on a nearby service track, but with 2-13 approaching the station, using that train's helper—its crew already at the controls—would hasten rescue.[24]

A brakeman disconnected hoses and lifted the cut lever. Conductor Clayton swung aboard, and the helper pulled away from 2-13 and entered the tunnel. Nosing up to the rear of the stranded train, Clayton had no trouble coupling it to the helper. However, he couldn't walk far enough forward to get to the mail car and loco to uncouple the rest of the train from them. After two failed attempts, he asked Stevens to try. Crawling on all fours to the mail car, Stevens uncoupled it from the train. The conductors signaled the helper, and Stevens rode out of the tunnel victoriously in the last car. As the helper pulled 1-13 out of the tunnel, it was switched onto the

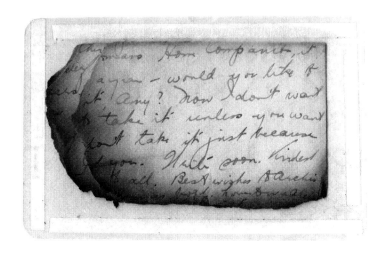

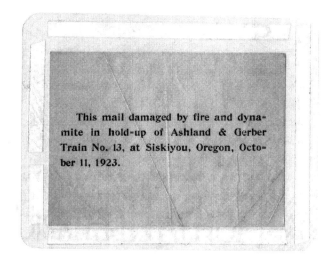

This mail damaged by fire and dynamite in hold-up of Ashland & Gerber Train No. 13, at Siskiyou, Oregon, October 11, 1923.

passing siding to free the mainline for 2-13 and other traffic. Unfortunately, bringing nearly one hundred coughing, panicky passengers out of the tunnel added to the confusion and anxiety.

If Micander disappeared a few minutes earlier, it's because he had taken on a rescue mission of his own. As far as anyone knew, the mail clerk had not been found yet and probably was still in the mail car. Micander knew there was a work crew with a locomotive about a mile west at White Point siding.

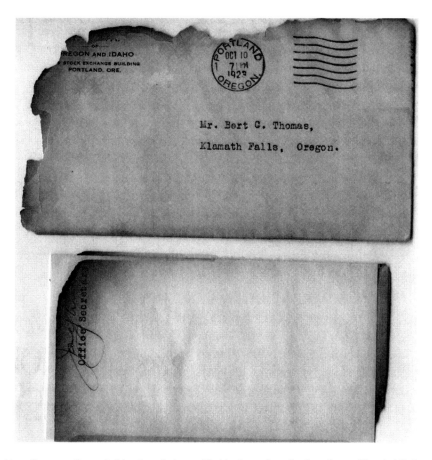

Above: Some mail, carried by the winds, avoided incineration. *Southern Oregon Historical Society Collection, #M34D, Box 1.*

Opposite: Roy used too much dynamite. The explosion and conflagration destroyed most of the mail in the car. *Southern Oregon Historical Society collect #M34D Box 1.*

He began to run and, reaching the siding, commandeered the engine, work crew and all fire extinguishers he could find. He stopped at the SP phone at the west end of the tunnel just long enough to get clearance to proceed with the work train. The blast having occurred about an hour earlier, No. 3626 had grown cold sitting on the mainline at the west portal. The work engine was made ready and coupled to No. 3626. It had begun to pull the loco and mail car out of the tunnel when the unexpected occurred.

There had been fires in the car following the explosion. Some had been extinguished; some had burned out. No one knew the state of the fires. Now, as the mail car was pulled out of the tunnel, movement and breeze caused a draft, and the fire reignited, causing a tremendous conflagration. Extinguishers were emptied. It was clear that neither the loco's fire hose nor workers shoveling sand and gravel into the flames could control this fire. The only thing to do was let the fire burn itself out.

Micander had hoped to find the mail clerk and save as much mail as possible. He failed with the mail; the only mail saved was that which had blown out of the car. He did succeed in finding Elvyn Dougherty. Under rubble in the mail car were remains of the U.S. mail clerk who had traded shifts.

MARY'S DIARY AND LIFE ALONG THE RIGHT-OF-WAY

Mary L. Hunter, wife of Edgar Hunter (engineer on the Shasta Division from 1906 until his death in 1931), was returning home from a trip to Portland during the attempted robbery. Edgar had been assigned to Ashland from 1910 until 1915, so the Hunters knew all the crewmen along the line:

October 10, 1923: I stopped at Ashland at 11:15 P.M. It was raining so I got a room at the Depot Hotel. I should have remained on the train.

October 11, 1923: Tunnel #13. Left Ashland on the 1ˢᵗ section of a long train. As we rode up the mountain, the sun was shining and everything was fresh and lovely after the rain. After we passed Siskiyou and were nearly to the end of Tunnel #13, the train began to go slower and slower and finally stopped. There was a terrific explosion and the sound of crashing glass that was frightening, but we did not know until hours later, when the Engine of the 2ⁿᵈ Section pulled us back to Siskiyou, that there had been an attempted hold-up, our Engineer Bates and Fireman Seng were shot to death, also Brakeman Johnson and the Mail Clerk. Never will I forget this day. I didn't really break until at Siskiyou I saw them carry Mr. Bates past our window. Then I cried hard. Some man said "Look at this woman, now she cries

[but] *in the tunnel she was the bravest in the car." He couldn't know of my Engineer husband and Fireman son. We left Siskiyou seven hours later.*

October 12, 1923: Home [Gerber, California] *at 6:15 this morning, after a sleepless night. Dad* [Edgar Hunter] *fixed some breakfast for me. It was good to be home after the horror of yesterday, and yet it will always be pleasant to remember the hour of trust and confidence that came to me with this verse: "The Eternal God is your salvation and underneath are the Everlasting Arms." The uncertain gloom of the tunnel was a sanctuary, trusting God in the face of unknown dangers. Before Dad went to work, at his request, I wrote to Mr. Fitzgerald* [at Southern Pacific headquarters in San Francisco] *to mention the brave thoughtfulness of three of his men when everything was confusion and people were hysterical with fright. I tried to sleep today but I keep going over the scenes of yesterday.*[25]

Mary Serena LaFlesh was born in 1866, oldest child of Thomas Jefferson LaFlesh, a Civil War captain of the Wisconsin Second Cavalry. The family relocated to Hornbrook, California, in 1888 when Thomas joined the Badger State Mining Company. Later, he became involved in the lumber business.

Mary wed John Cummings, a Shasta Division locomotive engineer, in 1892 and had three children: Kenneth, born in 1896 in Ashland; Thomas (or "Donald"), born in 1900 in Klamathon, California; and Dorine, born in Keswick, California, now under Lake Shasta. While living in Dunsmuir in 1906, Mary and John divorced, due mainly to his alcoholism.

Edgar Allen Hunter, born in Washington State in 1867 and widowed, also was an SP engineer and transferred from Rocklin, California, to Dunsmuir. Mary and Edgar married in 1907, and he raised the children as his own. During their twenty-four years together, the Hunters lived in Dunsmuir, Weed, Klamath Falls, Ashland, Redding, Red Bluff, Gerber, Alameda, Dorris, MacDoel and some towns more that once.

While living on B Street in Ashland's railroad district, Edgar and Mary developed whistle signals that would tell Mary if Edgar would be home soon or not for several hours. Such special or family whistle signals were common during the steam days when engineers could "play" their whistle chimes like musical instruments. Unfortunately, Edgar and Mary's signals are lost in time.

The Hunters were quite the railroad nomads, but it was the only life they knew, continually pulling up stakes and relocating. They would make the best of their many moves: rent a large house, rent out its rooms to supplement their railroad income, buy the house and then continue to rent out the rooms while the house increased in value.

In 1911, the Hunters were talked into buying a large house on the corner of Union and Fairview (117 Union) in Ashland. Although they felt they had paid too much for it, they enjoyed the many fruit trees that grew abundantly around the yard. They had chickens and bought milk from the Howards next door, and the schools were excellent.

In 1914, Mary rented the Imperial Arms boardinghouse. With the establishment not enjoying a stellar reputation in recent years, the city had closed it. To reopen, Mary named it Fairview Rooms and rented only to railroad men and families. In 1914, the Hunters rented a large home at 366 B Street, mainly for themselves, but Mary kept a few roomers for income.

Although the Great War ended in November 1918, the "great influenza" was just as devastating, affecting those in all walks of life. Engineer Frank O'Brien died, and Edgar bid O'Brien's local freight run between Redding and Gerber. Shortly thereafter, Edgar was diagnosed with the flu. It is questionable who was luckier: Ed for recovering or Mary for avoiding infection while tending to Edgar.

Frequently throughout those years and until she died in 1953, Mary would hop on a train with her pass to visit relatives and friends along the SP and Western Pacific Railroad lines (Mary's son Donald was an engineer on the WP). As a result of constant moving, there was no permanent home for Mary after Edgar's death from peritonitis in 1931. Instead, she would spend a year or so at a time with each of her children. Mary's family is grateful that she continued writing her diaries, as they are brief but insightful glimpses into the lives of so many. She shows with thoughtful writing that the life of a railroader is never easy, especially for families.

Chapter 5

MANHUNT AND CAPTURE

These officers, I guess they got cold feet. They turned back.
—Roy DeAutremont, June 1927

THE GETAWAY

Counting the missing mail clerk, four men were dead. The mail car was smoldering in the tunnel—it would be an hour before the boys could get into the car and start looking for valuables. By that time, posses and high-speed auto ambulances would begin arriving from Ashland. All was lost, and running was about all they could do. They made a beeline for their hideout and cache on the other side of Brushy Bald Mountain (about two miles west of the tunnel). There was no need to keep the three knapsacks they brought to carry loot. They took their weapons and flashlights but left everything else behind.

With the midday sun almost overhead, they became disoriented and argued about how to find the hideout. The farther they got from familiar geography near the tunnel, the more confused they grew. Pointing in different directions, Roy and Hugh each insisted that he knew the way. Roy gave in, and Hugh got them completely lost. Roy asked Hugh if he was satisfied now. Roy thought he could get them to the cache, and he did, just as it was getting dark. For some time, they listened to airplanes drone and circle overhead, surely searching for them. Most of the aircraft had been commandeered from the forest fire patrol.

The DeAutremonts were not alone. Hurrying to the scene were law officers and investigators from agencies near and far. Emergency equipment and staff were being staged in rail yards: hospital cars, wreckers and outfit cars. The railroad's investigative team was managed by Chief Special Agent Dan O'Connell of San Francisco. Most prominent of those assisting O'Connell were Dennis Quillinan, Charles Meyers and Ray Guilfoyle.

In charge of the U.S. Post Office Department's efforts was Chief Postal Inspector NW Charles Riddiford of Spokane. With the destruction of mail and a postal employee brutally murdered, the Post Office would be relentless in its pursuit of the criminals. Postmaster General Harry New told Riddiford to do whatever it would take to bring the murderers to justice. Assisting Riddiford were Ashland postal inspectors Arnold Brunner and George Houghen and Medford postmaster Bill Warner.

Active if not prominent in the investigation were Jackson County (Oregon) sheriff Charles Terrill and Siskiyou County (California) sheriff Andrew Calkins.

An Ashland detachment of thirty Oregon National Guard soldiers commanded by Captain Baker deployed early that evening and patrolled the Pacific Highway and abandoned roads until 2:00 a.m. the next morning.[1] As if that were not enough armament, it was hunting season, and there were hundreds of hunters in the hills. The boys were careful to stay out of sight. Their cache wasn't much more than a hole in the brush, but grateful for its protection, they stayed there for ten or twelve days.[2]

In the first few days after the murders, speculation regarding motives ran rampant. Perhaps the crime was just a bungled robbery attempt. With the mail car and contents incinerated (and railroad investigators tight-lipped), it would not be easy to determine what had been in the car. Hills nearby were filled with IWW members ("Wobblies") and other itinerants not fond of the SP and who sometimes used the Siskiyous for clandestine activities. Supposedly, there were officials of the American Legion onboard 1-13; they could have been targets of hostile labor groups. There was even rumor (unsubstantiated) that some of the trainmen that day had been strike-breakers during the recent, ugly SP labor dispute. Supposedly, this was their first scheduled run following the strike.[3]

Sometimes attempts to communicate seemed more hindrance than help. Everyone who thought they had seen the crooks phoned, cabled or wrote

The DeAutremonts were almost defensive, insisting that they left behind no evidence. In fact, even the detonator was in full view. *John Palmer photo, Southern Oregon Historical Society, #7918.*

The young criminals left unused knapsacks and creosote-soaked shoe covers a few yards up the hill from the track (lower middle in photo). *John Palmer photo, Southern Oregon Historical Society, #11106.*

Left: Chief Special Agent Dan O'Connell of San Francisco was in charge of Southern Pacific's investigation. *U.S. Post Office Department.*

Right: Chief Postal Inspector Northwest Charles Riddiford oversaw the territory he was responsible for from Spokane, Washington. *U.S. Post Office Department.*

Opposite: "Slaying in the Siskiyous" screamed headlines, circulars and posters everywhere. *U.S. Post Office Department.*

to any official involved in the investigation, asking for more information or expense money.

The revised plan was that Ray would sneak down the mountain, make it to Eugene somehow and then drive the Nash back along the Pacific Highway to a rendezvous near the cache. He had become a reasonably good driver in recent weeks. Would this work? There were still posses in the woods and airplanes overhead, but there were fewer signs of pursuit each day.

On the twelfth day after the holdup, the brothers shook hands, and Ray disappeared toward the railroad track, hoping for a quick trip to Eugene and back. To avoid capture, the boys would have to be careful but move fast—manage a speedy getaway down the Pacific Highway into California. Ray's pessimism returned: everything had gone wrong; the boys did not gain a dime from the caper, and they had killed three men, probably four; they were not just scared and crazy kids or common criminals—they were cold-blooded murderers.

Their luck grew worse that night: Ray's gun was not secure in his belt, and it fell to the track as he clambered into a gondola car of a slow-moving freight train. That reduced their firepower considerably; both Roy and Ray having lost their pistols, they were left with Ray's shotgun and Hugh's pistol. The gondola was empty except for a hobo also working his way north. Trying to engage Ray in small talk, the man asked him if he had heard about the SP train robbery two weeks earlier.

Ray rode the rails to Ashland and continued on foot to Medford. There, he walked into a restaurant and picked up a newspaper that seemed to scream, "Have you seen the DeAutremont Twins?" His spirits sank, and his heart stopped. Photos of the boys were printed all throughout the paper. Looking around, Ray was shocked to see their pictures on posters and circulars everywhere.

Forensics Wizard

The DeAutremont brothers were inept criminals. Their misuse of the dynamite was a good example. They needed only a few sticks to blow open the mail car door, but they used all the dynamite, incinerating the car and virtually cremating the mail clerk. Ray had some experience with explosives, but failing to supervise Roy, it was not evident. He did nothing to prevent the conflagration. Whether their increasing bad luck resulted from carelessness or stupidity, they did make mistakes and they did get discouraged, even to the point of discussing suicide. Ironically, it was Roy, destined to be a patient at the Oregon State Mental Hospital in later years, who talked Ray back "up" during his darkest moments. With Roy's optimism and adventurous young Hugh's swashbuckling manner, they kept going, foolish as they were. But it was not long before they met their match: Professor Edward Oscar Heinrich, a quiet chemistry teacher and scientist at the University of California–Berkeley who had come to be known as the "Edison of Crime Detection."[1]

The Siskiyou country was combed again and again by hundreds of armed searchers looking for the criminals. The first few days of the manhunt slipped away, and investigators of the Post Office, railroad and law enforcement found no significant clues. The stolen detonator was hard to trace because there was delay in reporting the theft. The pistol that Roy dropped was

Top: As a chemist and professor at the University of California–Berkeley, Edward Oscar Heinrich was known by some as the "Wizard of Berkeley." *Oakland Tribune*.

Bottom: The crime solver—the "smoking gun" in the DeAutremont identification—turned out to be a pair of coveralls sent to Professor Heinrich for analysis. *Terry Skibby*.

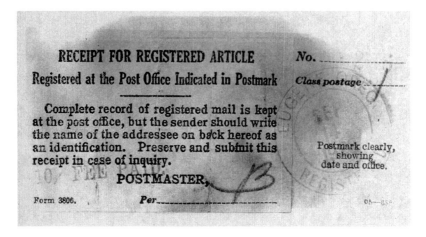

Carefully reexamining the coverall's pockets, Heinrich found a criminologist's treasure-trove. *U.S. Post Office Department.*

When Ray snuck down the mountain hoping to retrieve their Nash, he was shocked to find DeAutremont wanted posters everywhere. *Smithsonian National Postal Museum.*

recovered, but it was purchased with an alias and visible serial numbers had been filed away. Neither would creosote-soaked shoe covers, three knapsacks, two canteens or a few utensils left behind do much to solve the crime quickly.

SP's Dan O'Connell and the Post Office's Charles Riddiford had worked successfully with Professor Heinrich before; they did not hesitate to bring him into the Siskiyou crime. Among the first items sent to Heinrich was a set of coveralls found near the west tunnel portal. With the garment handled over and over, investigators were sure that it contained nothing of value and no evidence. But Heinrich started over inspecting evidence and amazed investigators with a preliminary report: "Look for a left-handed lumberjack who's worked around fir trees. The man you want is white, between 23 and 25 years of age, not over 5 feet 10, and he weighs about 165 pounds. He has medium light brown hair, a fair complexion, small hands and feet, and is rather fastidious in his personal habits. Apparently he has lived and worked in the Pacific Northwest."[5]

Professor Heinrich based these findings largely on what he found in pockets, overlooked earlier, and studied under his microscope. Fine sawdust came from Douglas fir trees such as are found in western Oregon's forestlands. Hairs could be matched under the microscope with those found on other items. What looked like grease spots on the overalls were actually pitch from fir trees. He felt that the owner was left-handed from wear mark patterns on the sides of the garment.

As it turned out, Heinrich was wrong on two counts: none of the DeAutremonts was left-handed, and none of the boys ever weighed more than 135 pounds. But Heinrich kept producing more details, and his forensic skills astounded those with whom he worked. Investigators changed their approaches and limited their searches, as suggested by Heinrich's findings. If he could be criticized for two small errors, then he was exonerated a couple days later when he named the criminals.

Found near the detonator, the overalls clearly were part of the crime (the boys used them to conceal and carry the detonator to the tunnel). Professor Heinrich was going over the garment one more time when he found a small piece of paper crumpled in the bottom of the overalls' pencil pocket. It was a U.S. Post Office Department registered mail receipt for fifty dollars sent from a "Roy d'Autremont" (as the boys sometimes spelled their name around this time) in Eugene, Oregon, to "Verne d'Autremont" in Lakewood, New Mexico. Investigators rushed to father Paul's home in Eugene, hoping to find clues to the boys' whereabouts. Paul confirmed that they sometimes used his address and explained that he was worried—the boys were late returning from a hunting trip.

Gun found at end of tunnel where it was dropped by one of the bandits boarding train previous to the holdup.

As Roy and Hugh scurried to board the locomotive tender, Roy's Colt .45-caliber automatic pistol fell to the track. *U.S. Post Office Department.*

The "Wizard of Berkeley" continued investigating. Finding duplicate registration numbers hidden inside the Colt .45 pistol (no. 130-763), he established that the weapon dropped onto the track was registered in Roy's handwriting to "William Elliot," one of Ray's aliases. Hairs from the coveralls matched hairs on a red sweater of Roy's left in Paul's home. Now, after eleven days of research, investigators and law officers had names and knew who to look for. The manhunt would continue for three and a half years and run up costs of about $500,000.[6] Without Professor Heinrich's modern methods of criminal investigation, the eventual cost would have been far greater.

Risking detection every moment, Ray needed to avoid scrutiny. But being broke, hungry and without a weapon, he had to make a little pocket money before attempting to return to his brothers in the hideout. Trying to stay out of sight, he walked to the little town of Central Point, twenty-seven miles north of the crime scene and got a job picking apples in the orchard of Dave Finley.[7] Room and board were included in the work.

Above: "REWARD! Kindly Place in a Conspicuous Place!" *U.S. Post Office Department.*

Left: "FOUR MEN MURDERED!" *Southern Oregon Historical Society, #17051.*

Surrounded by men looking for him, Ray had a close call with Finley. Eyeing Ray from head to toe, Finley started to reach for something in his pocket, like a wanted circular. But just as quickly, he stopped and called for his wife to bring him his sheepskin coat. With great show, Finley strapped on a gun belt, shoved his gun into its holster and strode out the door to go chase the DeAutremonts—all while Ray sat in Finley's house.

Continuing to Eugene to retrieve the car was no longer an option. Ray certainly would have been discovered. Day and night, radio broadcasts repeated the DeAutremonts' story and identification. Airplanes dropped leaflets over remote areas. After picking apples for a few days, Ray tucked away his meager earnings and headed for the nearest train stop. Another close call came when Ray rode the cushions back to Ashland: he had to maintain composure while a chatty brakeman recounted the whole holdup story to him.

Amazingly, Ray returned to the mountain. Against the odds, he found in the black of night the hideout that the brothers had trouble finding in daylight. Roy praised Ray's loyalty; he didn't have to come back to the cache, risking capture and death, but he did.

CHOICES AND DECISIONS

On his aborted mission to get the Nash, Ray learned that the authorities had identified the boys, and posters offered rewards of $4,800 apiece, dead or alive. Folks seemed to discuss nothing but the crime, and the prevailing belief was the boys soon would be caught and hanged. It was just a matter of time. Thinking about dying at the end of a rope, Ray had had enough: "Boys, life has dealt me its last dirty blow—I'm going to be leaving you."

Roy knew that this meant Ray was considering suicide. Roy didn't want to give up yet and had more influence over Ray than anyone. In later years, Roy explained, "Something in me made me want to put it to the test—to a contest. I wanted to see, with all the odds there were against us if we couldn't make it." He appealed to his twin, "Ray, let's fight it out to the end and maybe they won't get us."

Roy asked Hugh and Ray to stay with him. Hugh was willing, but Ray resisted. Roy credited his influence over Ray for finally getting him to stay.[8]

When Ray returned to the cache, he had brought a few raisins and other staples. The boys watched their supplies dwindle and knew that they soon would be out of food. They discussed leaving the cache. Roy thought that it was October 29 when they departed, striking out west toward the Oregon coast. They planned to advance cautiously and take all the time they would need—maybe six months. Cold campfires and tracks reminded the boys that there still was a very active manhunt underway. For three days, they hiked west. On one of these days, the brothers climbed a small hill that was quite bare. Suddenly, a number of airplanes seemed to come from nowhere and flew low, straight at them. The boys dove for brush cover and didn't know if they had been seen or not. Clearly, these infernal machines would hamper their getaway; they seemed to buzz the sky every day.

Each night, the boys built a small campfire, trying to stay warm. They understood the dangers but knew that they would die without a little heat. From exposure, lack of food and being confined to the cache for so long, their bodies had lost much strength. It was difficult, but they managed to carry ammunition and their guns: the twelve-gauge shotgun and one .45-caliber pistol.

Just as it began to snow lightly, the brothers stumbled into a small cabin. They cooked beans they found inside. What they did not eat that evening they cooked again the next morning. Roy noted later that they always seemed to have "a little grub," but it never was enough to sustain them. Although it was still snowing, they sensed that they were dangerously close to California logging camps and needed to move on.

They decided that they would strike out to the west again. But the beans digested, and the boys' gnawing hunger returned. Tramping the hills all day, they shot at a few deer but wasted the ammunition. Now it was almost dark. They knew that they could not continue this way and make the coast, so they discussed options. It seemed that the only way to survive was to double back to a logging road and then walk out to find food. They slept on the ground that night next to a large campfire to survive.

By morning, they had lost most of their body strength and could not carry even the blankets that had been their bedrolls. They kept their two guns but left most of the ammunition behind. They had just enough strength to approach a logging camp and get their bearings so they would be able to find the road that night and walk out. Not far from the camp, they found a deserted cabin near a creek. From a neglected vegetable garden, they picked lettuce, turnips and onions and carried this bounty into the cabin. They built a fire in the fireplace. Had they not been so tired, they would have worried when a man on foot passed the cabin and seemed to take note of the chimney smoke. There was activity around them; other cabins seemed occupied. But the brothers were too exhausted to care. They collapsed in front of the cabin's fireplace and slept all day.

Just before dark, they set out to find the logging road. As they walked south alongside what appeared to be a lumber camp commissary, Ray and Hugh invited themselves inside and purloined a hind quarter of veal and a large slab of bacon. The brothers ate much of the bacon raw on the spot. They continued down the road and found a quiet place in the brush where they tried to sleep, but it was too cold. They cooked some of the veal and bacon. It helped, but their strength did not return. They had trouble keeping track of time, but that did not seem important.

The next day, after dark, the brothers continued down the road toward Hilt, a busy Fruit Growers Supply Company mill town. Before stopping for the night, they advanced far enough so that they would be able to reach Hilt in a few hours the next night. They would have to go through Hilt to continue their escape.

The following day, the travelers stepped down off the road into a brushy area just before Hilt. The weather was miserable—rain, sleet and snow. They built a fire and cooked more of the meat. Roy and Ray still carried a small kit of barbering tools: scissors, clippers, razor and comb. They got these out and did the best two barbers could do to clean up three tramps. Roy said later that Ray and Hugh "had some pretty decent clothes..," but that has to be doubted with their sleeping on the ground. They had planned to walk south along the SP track to get away from Hilt (and scrutiny) as quickly as possible. But taking this route, they found themselves getting closer to the depot than they wanted to be.

Suddenly, automobile headlights switched on, illuminating the brothers. Voices called out to stop. The boys figured that these were Hilt police officers who must have recognized them as the DeAutremonts. The boys could not turn around, and they could not stop. Roy was unarmed, so Ray told his twin to go on ahead of them. Roy turned off the track, and they followed him into the brush. Roy thought that they were trapped, but something surprising happened: the lawmen stopped. They didn't pursue them. Evidently, no one was eager for a confrontation and a shootout. The boys did not run but walked fast through the brush and got separated for a while. Roy saw the silhouettes of two men up ahead on the track and feared that they were the officers. Fatigued and careless, he decided to take a chance and call out to them. It turned out they were Ray and Hugh.

The weather got steadily worse—a cold wind, rain and snow. Just below (south of) Hilt, they dropped down into a drainage culvert, built a small fire and ate a little bacon and veal. They agreed that they could not go back into the brush: with the miserable, wet weather, the brush no longer protected them. Why wasn't the law, if that is who they were, chasing them? Again, the boys reasoned that the officers did not want to die in a shootout, but neither did they want to lose their jobs later for not "sounding the alarm." It was best for the policemen to pretend that nothing had happened.

Ray talked again about giving up, turning themselves in and ending it all. His mood was one of deep, constant melancholia. He was sure that the officers must have telephoned the next railroad town, Hornbrook, to be on the lookout for the DeAutremonts. Surely they would be captured soon. As tempting as giving up may have sounded, Roy would have none of it. Again, he persuaded Ray not to quit, and Hugh agreed to continue on. They nearly froze to death that night and could hardly walk or move by morning. They spent the day in the culvert and didn't build a fire until late in the day. They decided to get rid of the shotgun, leaving it there in the culvert because it was too difficult to carry and conceal.

Near dark, they started down the track near the Pacific Highway. People along the Highway saw the brothers but did not seem interested. Encouraged, they built a fire and cooked a little more meat before disappearing into the darkness. They walked the track to Hornbrook, a busy little twenty-four-hour railroad town at the base of the Siskiyous, important as a helper locomotive terminal. With his shave and haircut a few days earlier and wearing an overcoat, Ray looked pretty "cleaned up." He went into Hornbrook ahead of the other two and visited a small confectionery store. His total wealth now was fifteen cents, but he spent all of it on three five-cent pieces of candy. Everyone in the store seemed to be discussing the "tunnel robbery." He listened for a while and then slipped out the door to meet up with Roy and Hugh.

Each dining on his piece of candy, they left Hornbrook by highway rather than rail. They walked until midnight, ducking off the highway whenever a vehicle approached. Building a fire, they finished the meat and spent the rest of the night trying to sleep on river rocks on the bank of the Klamath River. The next day, they would make one of their biggest decisions.

DOWN THE HIGHWAY

This would be tough. The young DeAutremont brothers had been through much together and were emotionally very close. The idea of separating wrenched at their heartstrings, but the decision might save their lives. They did not know quite what to expect, but they would try to stay in touch. For a start, they would write to one another at the Santa Ana, California Post Office in thirty days. If for some reason they could not make contact, they would meet at the largest YMCA in New York City on January 1, 1928.

Communicating could be dangerous and complicated, so they would avoid their real names and use aliases instead: "William R. Elliott" (Ray), "Johnie (or Johnny) Johnson" (Roy) and "James C. Price" (Hugh).[9] As in their earlier writings, they used "J" names and even the name "James" (especially Hugh and Roy) to honor their boyhood idol, Jesse James. Hugh was careless and flagrant in his hero worship. After running into the cow on September 26 (before the holdup), he had to remain three nights in Ashland while the Park Garage awaited parts to repair the car. Wary, he changed his lodging each day—the Fairview Rooming House, the Park Hotel and the Gurna Rooming House—but he used the name "E.E. James" throughout his stay, not bothering to change it.[10] During the manhunt, it would be fairly easy for investigators to follow the DeAutremonts' "trail of Js."

Ray was the first to leave. They shook hands and spoke a few words, and then Ray began walking south down the Pacific Highway, not a penny to his name. He thought about what his life had become, about the choices he had made. An hour later, Roy and Hugh left together, also broke. Still near the Klamath River, they came to where some men were spearing large, plentiful salmon. Roy approached and asked one of the fishermen if he would give him a salmon. Seeing Roy bedraggled and hungry, the man gave him a big fish. He and Hugh set off down the highway, Roy holding the great fish by the gills and dragging its tail on the road. The boys walked all day.

That evening, they found an abandoned highway construction camp and, inside, a small container of syrup. Roy went to a nearby house and asked the occupant for bread. He got biscuits and traded some with a tramp on the highway for coffee. Roasting their salmon and heating the biscuits and coffee, Roy and Hugh enjoyed their first real meal in many weeks. With the wind blowing cold, they couldn't sleep that night, but the hearty meal kept them from freezing.

Early that morning, they finished what they had not eaten and started down the highway again. Sometime that day, an automobile stopped, and the driver gave the boys a ride to Yreka, California. Roy was very self-conscious. Sleeping on the ground and huddling next to campfires, he was sure that he looked worse than any tramp. Taking a walking tour of Yreka, the boys noticed townsfolk paying a lot of attention to them. It was time to move on.

With an early start the next morning, they walked down the highway and reached the little farming community of Granada. They watched a farmer haying in his field, and Roy motioned him to the fence. He asked the farmer if he needed any hired help. Farmer Bill Johns said yes, and he wanted to hire both Roy and Hugh. Getting Hugh off on the side, Roy explained why they could not both work for Johns: two boys, too suspicious. Roy offered to Hugh that Hugh take the job, and Roy would continue on to find other work. Adventuresome Hugh declined, wanting Roy to take the job and Hugh would continue on. Careful to show no emotion or relation, Hugh ambled down the highway, and Roy stayed. This was the last time Roy would see Hugh as a free man.

Roy (now alias "Clarence H. Dodgeworth") worked for Johns for a few weeks. During that time, Johns's family, hired hands and fellow Mormon churchmen discussed the Siskiyou tunnel crime constantly. Roy began to get interested in the Mormon faith and attended meetings. But he was bothered by the questions folks were asking, like where he was when the crime occurred. They asked "Clarence" if that young boy he had been walking with the day he hired on was his brother. Roy quickly denied any tie, saying that he was just a bum he had never seen before.

A money problem developed. Johns owed Roy wages but did not particularly want to part with the money. Roy found that he had somewhat of a deadbeat reputation around the Shasta Valley. One afternoon, Johns had a number of visitors at the house. Roy brought up the money he was owed. Johns said that he did not have that much cash around the house, and if he were to write a check, it could not be cashed until the next day. Roy told him to write a check anyway and said that he would take his chances with it. Roy took the check to the biggest store in Granada and cashed it to buy ten dollars worth of clothes. He then registered at a local hotel and asked to be awakened in time to catch the next day's 2:31 a.m. westbound California Express.

Granada was a flag stop for No. 15, not a scheduled stop. It was exceptionally foggy that morning, and the engineer evidently did not see the newspaper that Roy had rolled up and lit to use as a flag. The train did not stop. Roy walked back to the hotel for a little more sleep. At about 6:00 a.m., he rose again and set out to walk the Pacific Highway all day. He daydreamed about palm trees and California's balmy weather, but travel would be difficult for a while.

Bundled against the cold and snow, he walked and hitchhiked out of the Shasta Valley and down the Sacramento River Canyon. One wonders how easily he passed through Dunsmuir, where grieving family and angry railroaders had recently buried Fireman Marvin Seng. He hitched and walked for three days and came to the good-sized town of Redding, California. Checking job boards, the only work he found was cutting cordwood, and he did not have his own tools, as was required. He continued alongside the Pacific Highway to Sacramento. Shortly after arriving, he fell ill for a few days.

Barely able to move, Roy did manage to find an affordable housekeeping room at the Bachelors' Hotel. Checking job boards in Sacramento was no more promising than in Redding. He had hoped to recover and stay put until he could write to Ray and Hugh in Santa Ana; the thirty days until they'd attempt to communicate was about up. But his money did not hold out, and the rent was due. Since he could not pay it, he moved out. He hung around Sacramento for a while but decided that no one, seeing him sick and puny, would hire him. Distracting him momentarily was a meeting of Spiritualists in Sacramento. Still interested in matters of faith, Roy attended the meeting and was somewhat attracted to their teachings.

From his purchases back in Granada, Roy had some nice, clean logger's clothing. But he felt that he or his clothing was drawing too much attention; perhaps he had detectives watching him.[11] He spent a night in a rooming house and then left Sacramento the next day. A job pruning grapes fifteen miles away lasted only two days before Roy was fired. On the road again, he felt safe from detectives for the moment, thinking that he must be a step ahead of them. He was eager to get the address of the Santa Ana Post Office so he could communicate with Ray and Hugh. An automobile stopped, and the driver offered Roy a ride to Vacaville, California, saying that it was a good town with work prospects as good as anywhere. Roy accepted the ride and decided that he would stay in Vacaville until he could communicate with Ray and Hugh.

Roy got a job on the Uhl Ranch. Using the name he had selected on the banks of the Klamath River a month earlier, "Johnie Johnson," he wrote to his brothers in Santa Ana. He did not get letters back at first. He never heard from Hugh, but Ray had received Roy's letter and quickly wrote back to him in Vacaville. Roy took comfort reading nothing in the papers about capture of the other two. And there was always the boys' secondary plan of meeting at the largest YMCA in New York City on January 1, 1928.

In the meantime, also migrating south in California, Ray had done better than Roy—better jobs and better wages. This was no surprise to Roy, who still regarded himself as puny. Delighted to be in touch with Roy again, Ray sent him money two or three times using the name "Carlson." Roy wrote to Ray asking that he come up to Vacaville for a visit. Arranging to meet after dark, Roy was amazed by how fit Ray looked. Last together nearly three months earlier, Ray looked about starved then and had emaciated facial features. Now, he was as well and strong as Roy had ever seen him. The twins talked long into the night, taking care not to be seen.

Ray decided that he would travel to Detroit. He got another job and earned enough to go east. He must have ridden the rods rather than the cushions, though, because he told how he had to "walk the gauntlet...go through a double line of officers" in both Denver and Chicago.[12] But Ray got through these hobo roundups without trouble. Changing his alias to "Jimmie Williams," he got a job quickly in a Detroit foundry.

Back in Vacaville, Roy continued to work for Uhl for $2.50 per day, without board. He tended to shy away from the post office because the postmaster had neatly arranged a "regular rogues' gallery," as Roy called it. Roy was one of the rogues. One day, the boys from the ranch were uptown, and one wanted to go into the post office to mail a letter. In a moment of lunacy, Roy decided to go in with him, to see if he could get in and out without detection. The ranch hand stopped Roy right beside his poster. Then he began to read and study the poster directly above Roy's: Harry J. Dunlap, arrested in Detroit for robbery, rape and murder. There certainly was a likeness. The coincidence was closer than Roy felt comfortable with; he suggested they go get a drink, and the hand was first out the door.

Working for Uhl, Roy discovered that several of his hired hands were ex-convicts—solid workers but one-time criminals. Roy asked one to send away for a mail-order German Luger for him. Roy was carrying this pistol when he was arrested.

Back East

Ray sent money to Roy several more times trying to coax him to come east and join him in Detroit. After six months, Roy agreed. Catching a train to Chicago on or about July 4, 1924, he made a connection to Detroit, checked into the Roosevelt Hotel and met Ray outside the next morning. He began looking for a job, but a problem occurred. He was wearing dark glasses to obscure the marked likeness he bore to his circular photos. Dark glasses were commonplace in California, but not in Detroit. He noted that detectives were watching him, but they all seemed to "let me alone."[13] After a day or two, an employment agency found a job for Roy washing dishes at a small hotel in South Alliance, thirty or forty miles from Detroit.

The "detective problem" seemed to get worse. Watching him more and more, Roy said that they were burning him up with their eyes. Roy said that a boy living at the hotel asked him, "Johnie, what are all those detectives doing at this hotel?" They seemed to be everywhere, and Roy watched them carefully. Certain that they knew who he was, Roy hatched a scheme to blow the detectives' cover with a false crime plan. He wrote to Ray, suggesting that he "get Hugh up here at once and pull that job we were planning on." No "detectives" reacted, and Ray had no idea what Roy was writing about. The next day, Roy went fishing, and the day after that, he got fired. He collected his wages and went back to Detroit.

Still confused, Ray thought that they ought to get out of town quickly. He left his wages behind, and the two started walking. Canada was so close that they thought it might be their best bet for escape. But before they could figure out where and how to cross the Detroit River, other problems surfaced. A new series of circulars was blanketing the border, and rumrunners were dangerous in the area. They decided that trying to cross into Canada was not a good plan. Surely they would be picked up or risk injury.

Ray favored a plan that would get them to New Orleans and then onto a steamer to the Orient—kind of a vague scheme. They had heard that there was an island, Ocracoke, off the North Carolina coast that was considered a safe place for criminals to hide out. Walking south, they set out for Ohio. They caught a freight and rode the rails as far as Wellston, Ohio.

Talking with folks there, they learned that West Virginia could be a tough state to get through. Locals also warned of difficulty getting to and living on Ocracoke; maybe that was not such a good place to live after all. Someone recommended that they consider Ironton, Ohio, on the Kentucky border. On a whim, they tried it. Disappointed that there was no work there, they found a shanty not far from town and stocked it with groceries. Maybe more important than work, this could be a good place to lay low until detectives lost interest and things quieted down. Although Roy said that he was not up to working, the brothers did cut railroad ties and do odd jobs for the locals.

After a while, they moved to Sulphur Springs, Ohio, where Ray met and married sixteen-year-old Hazel Sprouse in August 1925. A pretty neighborhood girl, Hazel was a daughter of timber cruiser James Sprouse and his wife, Jane. For years, it would be said that Ray married Hazel only to obscure his identity—just as he had bleached his hair nearly blonde and convinced a dentist to remove a supposedly painful front tooth. The boys

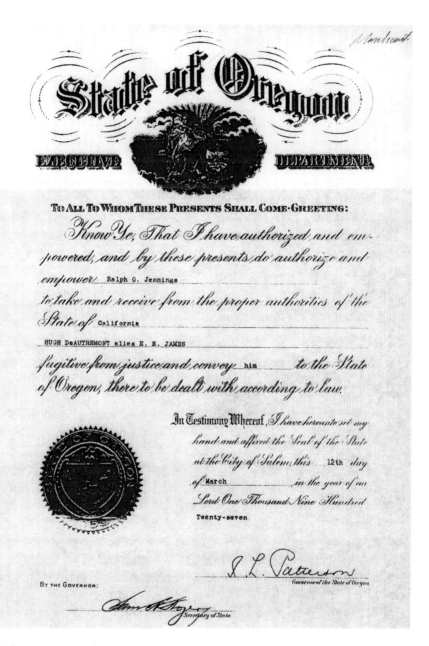

State of Oregon

EXECUTIVE DEPARTMENT

TO ALL TO WHOM THESE PRESENTS SHALL COME-GREETING:

Know Ye, That I have authorized and empowered, and by these presents do authorize and empower Ralph G. Jennings

to take and receive from the proper authorities of the State of California

HUGH DeAUTREMONT alias E. E. JAMES

fugitive from justice and convey him *to the State of Oregon, there to be dealt with according to law.*

In Testimony Whereof, I have hereunto set my hand and affixed the Seal of the State at the City of Salem, this 12th *day of* March *in the year of our Lord One Thousand Nine Hundred* Twenty-seven

L. L. Patterson
Governor of the State of Oregon

BY THE GOVERNOR:

Secretary of State

With Oregon governor Patterson's signature, Hugh was extradited to Oregon. *Jackson County Circuit Court Archives.*

still used aliases, so Hazel knew her new husband only as "Elmer Goodwin." Roy took the name of "Clarence Goodwin."

With the twins seeking work that winter, Hazel accompanied Ray ("Elmer") to Portsmouth, Ohio, and Washington, Ohio. They left Roy ("Clarence") behind. When spring came, Roy went to West Virginia and worked for a while in the coal mines. While Roy was in the mines, Ray came back to Pine Grove, Ohio (which they came to consider as "home"), and stayed until Roy returned. The boys worked together during the summer months. In the fall, they found work together in Hanging Rock, Ohio, tearing down an old smokestack for Hanging Rock Coal and Iron Company.

Ray and Roy enjoyed a good life in Ohio. They had reasonable jobs, made a little money, paid their debts and made friends. Ray treated his young wife with nothing but respect. Work opportunities continued. Roy quit his job at Hanging Rock and worked in a coal mine near McKeevey, West Virginia, for two and a half months. He quit that job and returned to Pine Grove to enjoy time with Ray, Hazel and their new baby, Jackie Hugh, during the holidays. After Christmas, Roy went to Steubenville, Ohio, with two friends: Ora Brumfield and Arthur Marshall.

Roy was doing well in Steubenville, and Ray wanted to join him. Roy consented. Ray sold what he owned in Pine Grove and moved his family to Steubenville, where he took a job working in a mill. With Ray's family resettled, Roy stayed in Pine Grove for a few weeks to relax with friends. Wandering the neighborhood, he noticed several copies of a new DeAutremont poster and circular. There were only two faces on it; Hugh's was conspicuously absent. Roy hurried to Ray's house. He told Ray about Hugh and noted that the twins' new photos were particularly revealing. Ray's looked just like him.

After a long discussion, the boys decided that they were not safe in Ohio; they would have to make a run for Mexico. But what about Hazel and baby Jackie? Taking them to Mexico would introduce a new set of challenges. It would take them two additional months to earn the $700 (at least) they would need to take Ray's family with them to Mexico. Staying in Mexico would be difficult, especially for Hazel. Would she reveal clues that would give them away? Ray was inclined to take the family; Roy did not ask him not to. They were torn.

Arthur Marshall and Roy were sitting in the employment office one day. They had come down that morning to see if they could get mill jobs to get out of the mines. The clerk seemed to recognize Roy. He disappeared for about fifteen minutes. When he returned, he was accompanied by the chief

Above, left: Serving together in the U.S. Army and Philippine Islands, Thomas Reynolds saw a wanted poster in which private "Jimmy Price" looked remarkably like fugitive Hugh DeAutremont. *U.S. Post Office Department.*

Above, right: Albert Collingsworth worked briefly with the "Goodwin" brothers near Steubenville, Ohio. *U.S. Post Office Department.*

Left: Emma Maynard gathered information she had on the "Goodwin" brothers and contacted federal investigators. *U.S. Post Office Department.*

of police, Ross Cunningham, and two other armed officers. There was no place to run, nothing to do. Roy knew that the manhunt was over for him.

The twins' concerns about Hugh were justified: he indeed had been arrested. Following the brothers' escape from the Siskiyous and splitting up in northern California, Hugh made his way to Santa Ana, where the boys had agreed they'd use mail and aliases to rendezvous. When they failed to make contact, Hugh hung around Los Angeles and Long Beach and then decided to go into Mexico. He was able to speak Spanish, and he thought there would be less interest in him there. But that was not the case: after a few weeks, a new issue of wanted posters and circulars flooded Mexico. He returned north to Mexicali, passed through Yuma and El Paso (where he was unsuccessful finding a girl he once knew) and briefly considered going home to New Mexico.

Hugh was feeling the pressure—wanted posters were everywhere. He was haunted by recollections of the locomotive's bell ringing incessantly. He could not shake the image of the dying brakeman, imploring, "Wait a minute, boys!" He had to keep moving, riding the rails. In Arkansas, he worked briefly for Bill Adams. Hugh was struck in the eye by a wedge but recovered his sight. He returned to Santa Ana just on the chance that he'd find his brothers hanging around the post office. Unable to find them, he eventually hopped freight trains to Chicago.[14]

Using his alias "James C. Price," Hugh enlisted in the army in April 1924, six months after he shot Sid Bates in the head. He was detailed to foreign service and arrived in Manila in 1925. Assigned clerical work for skills he had acquired in high school, he was known to military buddies as "Jimsey." Then, Thomas Reynolds, Hugh's sergeant in the Philippines, saw a wanted poster in San Francisco, and its image of Hugh looked just like "Price." Reynolds contacted postal investigators, and Hugh was arrested at Los Banos, Philippine Islands, on February 11, 1927, as a private in Company B, Thirty-first Infantry.[15] He was returned to San Francisco on the steamer *Thomas* in March, turned over to Oregon authorities and charged with first-degree murder.[16] At the time of his arrest, Hugh was twenty-three years old. Reynolds, who put investigators on to Hugh, received $5,300 of the $15,900 total reward.[17]

Following Hugh's arrest, there was greatly increased interest in the DeAutremonts and their crime. An elderly man living in Portsmouth, Ohio, Albert Collingsworth, studied recent accounts and thought that he recognized the twins as the Goodwin brothers. He had worked with the boys briefly at Hanging Rock. He called a detective agency, which in turn contacted the Post Office Department and the U.S. Bureau of Investigation, predecessor of the Federal Bureau of Investigation.

Authorities set a trap for the twins—they posted notices that there were a few better-paying jobs available at a mill on the other side of town. When Roy showed up at the personnel office, he was arrested quietly without incident. In the meantime, Ray was at home sleeping prior to a work shift. Officers came to his door and told Hazel that "Clarence" (Roy) had been injured on the job and hospitalized. Hazel awakened Ray, and he dressed quickly. As they left the house, officers surrounded and arrested Ray on less than amicable terms. He was said to have growled to officers, "You got me at last. You're lucky you didn't come upstairs or I'd have used my automatic. I never intended to be taken alive."

The twins admitted using false names but denied having anything to do with a train robbery or—worse—murder. Cooperative after Ray's "toot," both twins agreed to be extradited to Oregon and transported to Jacksonville for indictment. Collingsworth received $1,700 for his role in the twins' arrest.[18]

Newspaper accounts noted that the twins "continued in high spirits" while they were held briefly in Steubenville as arrangements were made to move them to Oregon. One account reported them "singing French songs" in their cell as curious crowds listened. This surprised Ray in later years: he said that they spoke some Spanish but no French until studying it in prison years later.[19]

Also later, Ray told interviewers that the toughest part of the ordeal for him was seeing his family, Hazel and little Jackie Hugh, just before leaving Steubenville. Hazel, pregnant again, was completely confused by events and stories about her husband's true identity. "Ray"? "Elmer"? What was she to believe? In her visit to Ray's cell to say goodbye, she held up Jackie to the bars, and he reached out for Ray to take him. But when the little fellow realized that the bars prevented his daddy from holding him, he began to cry. Ray said later, "I was choked up with emotion. Then my soul sank to zero." Just before Hazel left the jail, Ray asked a jailer for a copy of his "mug shot." On the back, he penned, "To my loving wife Hazel, because I love you. Take good care of Jackie and God bless your parents, Mom and Pop [Sprouse], Ray Charles DeAutremont." Ray may have married Hazel to help hide his identity, but clearly, he'd come to love her and their family.[20]

Notorious criminals, the brothers drew great crowds to the Steubenville jail. Nearly twenty thousand watched as Ray and Roy boarded their train in Ohio for Medford, accompanied by Jackson County sheriff Ralph Jennings, Deputy Louis Jennings and other law officers. The DeAutremont family's grief was by no means over. The train underway, the brothers were told that their "baby brother," Lee, had been accidentally killed in a pool hall incident in Crossett, Texas, and died on about March 2, 1927.[21] If the story of the DeAutremonts is one of wasted lives, then the death of youngest brother Lee must be included.

Form 1206-A

CLASS OF SERVICE DESIRED			NO.	CASH OR CHG.
DOMESTIC	CABLE			
TELEGRAM	FULL RATE			
DAY LETTER	DEFERRED		CHECK	
NIGHT MESSAGE	CABLE LETTER			
NIGHT LETTER	WEEK END LETTER		TIME FILED	

WESTERN UNION

Patrons should check class of service
desired; otherwise message will be
transmitted as a full-rate
communication.

NEWCOMB CARLTON, PRESIDENT   J. C. WILLEVER, FIRST VICE-PRESIDENT

Send the following message, subject to the terms on back hereof, which are hereby agreed to

Medford, Oregon, June 10, 1927.

William B. Bartels,
Assistant United States Attorney,
Columbus, Ohio.

Sheriff of Jackson County Oregon will claim Ray and Roy
De Autremont on State warrants charging first degree murder
and is leaving for Ohio with requisitions from Governor for
extradition of prisoners. Stop. When sheriff or deputy sheriff
presents warrants for said prisoners they should be released
to him for removal to Oregon to answer charges in the circuit
court of Jackson County Oregon. Stop. Am now engaged in trial
of Hugh De Autremont co-defendant of brothers held by you.

George Neuner,
United States Attorney for District
of Oregon.

Gov. Rate. Paid.
NIGHTDAY*
STRAIGHT MESSAGE.

Western Union assisted in the extradition of Ray and Roy from Ohio to Oregon.
Jackson County Circuit Court Archives.

Surrounded by lawmen, Roy (front) and Ray board the train in Steubenville for their
heavily escorted journey to Jacksonville *Terry Skibby.*

FATAL IRONY

Paul was disconsolate upon learning of his youngest son's death. "The father was so choked with emotion when he told of the telegram last night, that he was hardly able to speak….The sorrows of Job that have followed Mr. DeAutremont for three years were increased by this additional tragedy in his life."

Crossett, founded by Mrs. Minnie Crossett in October 1925, was a typical West Texas boomtown: not long after the rigs went up, Crossett boasted a post office, three hotels, a barbershop, a night club, several eating places, beer joints and a few houses. Oil field laborers worked hard and played harder.

What we know about that day is that while in a Crossett pool hall, Lee DeAutremont, age nineteen, was shot in the abdomen. Some time later—perhaps one day, maybe fourteen days—he died in St. John's Hospital in

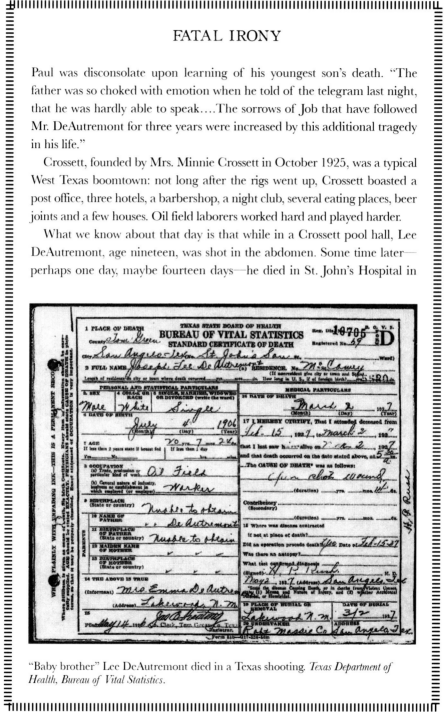

"Baby brother" Lee DeAutremont died in a Texas shooting. *Texas Department of Health, Bureau of Vital Statistics.*

San Angelo. Different sources reported different dates of the shooting and Lee's death. Law enforcement and newspapers seemed satisfied to accept Lee's killing as an "accident"; no one was eager to investigate another oil field killing. But clippings and Lee's death certificate led to interesting observations and an unsolved mystery.[22]

Lee's death certificate names "Mrs. Emma DeAutremont" as the "informant." Searching reveals no record of "Emma," and the several boxes on Lee's death certificate left blank suggest that she was not a close family member.

An unnamed companion transported grievously injured Lee 120 miles to San Angelo, but they could have driven only 40 miles to Odessa. Medical care was comparable. For someone suffering from a gunshot wound, bouncing over an extra 80 miles of road could have been a killer.

Interesting among date discrepancies are those involving Dr. Rush. The certificate reports that he operated on Lee on February 15, 1927, and then cared for the boy until he died on March 2. News articles reported that Lee was shot on February 25 and died four days later on March 1. It appears he was shot several days earlier than the papers reported.

It is possible that Lee's death was an accident as claimed, but there were interesting circumstances. For instance, at the time of his death, Lee was being watched by Mr. C.E. Thompson, special agent for the Kansas City, Mexico & Orient Railway.[23] Investigators hoped that his criminal brothers might try to contact Lee while he was still alive.

Mystery isn't the point of Lee's story, though; irony is. Earlier, on that infamous day in 1923, the first trainman to die was Coyl Johnson. DeAutremont brothers Ray and Hugh each shot Coyl. Three and a half years later, their brother Lee would die the same way: a shot to the gut.

Belle traveled to Texas to claim Lee's body and returned him to New Mexico for burial.[24]

Chapter 6

THE TRIAL

Those boys must pay. The DeAutremonts must pay and pay and pay as long as they live. Blood calls for blood and they will pay.
                                    —[father] *Paul DeAutremont, June 1927*

JACKSONVILLE

Hugh's arrest and long trip under military guard from Manila to San Francisco marked the beginning of the end of the DeAutremont brothers' freedom. The army detained him at the Alcatraz military prison while processing his extradition to Jackson County, Oregon. Hoping to glean information helpful in prosecuting Hugh, the county and SP offered to pay Belle's train fare from New Mexico to San Francisco and Medford. Eager to see young Hugh, Belle readily accepted what she naïvely regarded as a benevolent gesture.

Two other visitors to Alcatraz would soon play roles in Hugh's life: Jackson County sheriff Ralph Jennings and District Attorney Newton C. Chaney. Flamboyant Hugh, a small, wiry athlete, was a marked contrast to the veteran sheriff. Jennings was an older, silver-haired six-footer who didn't waste words, generally speaking only when he had something to say. The affable Hugh always regarded himself as able to "figure out" people, but

Chaney confused him. He was fairly quiet with Hugh, but the formidable glare of the steely-eyed district attorney made Hugh grateful that Chaney didn't prolong his visit.

On March 25, an army detachment turned over a manacled Hugh to Sheriff Jennings, and the two boarded the Southern Pacific for Oregon. Hugh, in a neat but well-worn blue serge suit, suddenly looked sullen and serious, a contrast to his youthful features and the straw hat he liked to wear at a rakish angle. He had a show to put on.

Dan Bowerman, city editor of the *Medford Daily News*, received a tip on the county's plan to move Hugh to Medford and Jacksonville. He bought a ticket and boarded the train at Hilt, a stone's throw from the California-Oregon border and Tunnel 13. Sheriff Jennings understood the power of the press (especially if the press was a city editor), so he agreed to let Bowerman interview Hugh after they arrived at Jacksonville. Jennings processed Hugh into the Jackson County Jail's single-occupant cell, the "Polly" on the second floor. The sheriff led him to the reception room and his interview with Bowerman. Hugh slouched in a chair irreverently and asked the reporter for a cigarette.

"This is better than that cell. That's a hell of a place, but I'm not complaining. I'm going to be a model prisoner."[1] Hugh talked about living at home with his mother in Artesia, near Lakewood, New Mexico. Graduating from Artesia High School just four months before the grisly murders, he was proud of his high school record: football quarterback, drama club member and captain of the track team. Handsome and gregarious, he was very popular in school. Hugh continued, "None of my friends who really know me will ever believe me guilty of the crime of which I am accused."

Bowerman asked, "Hugh, your Army time was about up. What did you intend to do after that?" The young actor looked up at the ceiling, paused and replied, "I wanted money. I have a little, but I was going to get a job, work until I had about two thousand dollars, then come back here and clear myself. I never dreamed of being captured, but I wanted to live under my right name, wanted the world to know I was innocent, and wanted my family to know it. I was coming back to clear my name, but this is just as well—except, of course, that I can't pay my lawyers until after I am turned free and can earn something."[2]

The interview was quite relaxed until Bowman asked what Hugh planned to use for an alibi. "On advice of my attorneys, I am saying nothing," the defendant declared.

Both Hugh's parents—Belle the storekeeper from Lakewood and Paul the paperhanger/barber from Eugene—arrived in Jacksonville the same day

During the first days of May 1927, automobiles line Jacksonville's streets and gawkers with lunch baskets fill the courthouse and grounds. *Southern Oregon Historical Society, #7586.*

Jackson County's courthouse was built in Jacksonville in 1883. *Southern Oregon Historical Society, #868.*

Jackson County's jail was adjacent to the courthouse. *Southern Oregon Historical Society, #2286.*

as Hugh, March 25, 1927. They had divorced ten years earlier, and Paul had remarried. Now, as their son was being locked up, they bumped into each other in the jail's courtyard and stoically shook hands. The scandal and drama were taking their toll on Paul: his conversation was erratic, and he was sometimes profane in defense of "my boy" Hugh. He was fit to bouts of mumbling, "My boys are not bad boys," and, "My boys are dead, buried by the real Siskiyou Bandits." Before the boys were captured and had confessed, Paul seemed to believe the lame story that the "real robbers" undoubtedly had killed the DeAutremont boys, possibly over "moonshine" liquor, and stolen their clothing. Paul would be of little to no help defending Hugh.

Normally strong and persevering, Belle showed great sadness in her face. Just a few weeks earlier, authorities had given her the terrible news that her youngest son, Lee, had been shot and killed "accidentally" in a poolroom incident in Texas. With Ray and Roy on the lam, only her oldest son, Verne, was living a normal, respectable life.

Bowerman reported that Hugh was "pleasant, confident, but not cocky."[3] Not all observers agreed. Some pointed to his straw hat, worn at a jaunty angle to acknowledge crowds of supporters and curious he encountered. In those first days of confinement in Jacksonville, Hugh walked with a swagger, a cigarette often hanging over his lip and showing occasional devil-may-care disdain for his captors. But that would change over the course of the lengthy trial. After a while, he looked exhausted and beaten down, even hopeless at times. In the courtroom, he seldom made eye contact with his parents.[4]

Paul's contribution to the trial was retaining attorney Fred Smith of Eugene for Hugh's defense. Smith, in turn, recruited John Collier of Portland, one of Oregon's most competent criminal attorneys. Gus Newbury, said to be the "dean of Medford's lawyers," rounded out the defense. Considering the publicity value of a DeAutremont trial, it may have surprised few that three such prominent attorneys would put on hold their busy, lucrative practices to defend Hugh. In press conferences, they claimed that they were happy to help an innocent lad find justice. Perhaps more surprising was that all three agreed to defend Hugh pro bono. Neither Hugh nor his family had money for legal fees.[5] Acts like these shed a positive light on the defense and made some wonder if Hugh actually might be innocent. Public sentiment shifted slightly in his direction.

The proceedings of Hugh's trial (actually two trials, including what would be a mistrial) were fascinating but confusing. The confusion began with the participants. This was a very high-profile trial because the state, the U.S. Post Office Department and Southern Pacific wanted the "supreme penalty" (death by hanging) in the worst way. In Oregon's judicial system in 1923, there were basically two jurisdictions or courts in which serious crimes could be tried: the circuit court (also called the state or county court) and the United States District Court (federal or U.S. court). U.S. courts generally heard cases that went beyond state lines. State courts, like the Jackson County Circuit Court, had jurisdiction over serious local crime, like murder. Sometimes, when jurisdiction was not clear, the courts would have to "work out" which one had jurisdiction. It is not difficult to imagine the sensitivity and disputes involving jurisdiction. Sometimes both federal and circuit courts had jurisdiction through different indictments, and that was the case in Hugh's trials.

Lawyers—judges, prosecutors and defense attorneys—come in all degrees of skill and experience. Some have political aspirations. When Hugh's trial began on May 2, 1927, there were no death penalties in the U.S. District Court that pertained to the circumstances of Hugh's accused crime. Those most eager for a hanging wanted a circuit court trial because murder (and some mail train crimes) fell into circuit court jurisdiction. The grand jury indicted Hugh on four counts of first-degree murder (the postal clerk and three trainmen) and on two lesser charges of interfering with a mail train. Very importantly, Hugh also was indicted on two federal charges of interfering with a mail train, but these were not part of the trial. A cagy prosecution convinced the U.S. District Court to seal the unspecified federal charges as "insurance" to help thwart possible future parole attempts. If Hugh were ever paroled, the federal indictment could be opened and used to throw him right back into jail.

Part of the sensitivity between courts was the idea that each should mind its own business, stay within its own jurisdiction. Why, then, did George Neuner, U.S. attorney for the District of Oregon, prosecute the circuit court case? And why did George Roberts, an accomplished and highly respected Medford attorney (who had been the Jackson County district attorney from 1916 to 1920), seemingly come back to the circuit court to help Neuner prosecute Hugh? Shouldn't District Attorney Newton Chaney have prosecuted the case?

Hugh's prosecutors were interesting personalities, and the processes through which they gained their positions were equally interesting. Judge and U.S. attorney vacancies in the U.S. District Court were filled by the president and approved by Congress. With turnover possible every four years, the U.S. attorney's job was prestigious but short-lived.

Positions like that of Jackson County district attorney Chaney were supposed to be filled by local elections. However, it happened that district attorneys often retired early, requiring a governor's appointee to fill the current term. This gave the appointee advantage in the next election and usurped the intended process.

The U.S. Post Office Department and the SP reminded everyone that they expected Hugh's conviction and a death penalty. As the Jackson County district attorney, Chaney was expected to prosecute Hugh. In fact, he did not. He sat at the table with the other prosecutors but was quiet during the trials. It was as if someone was not confident that Chaney could prosecute Hugh successfully and get the death penalty. To succeed, the prosecution needed someone with the talents and experience of George Neuner.

Neuner, a U.S. attorney, was prosecuting a state case outside his jurisdiction. However, that could be dealt with: the U.S. District Court approved a leave-of-absence for Neuner so he could accept temporary reassignment to the circuit court. Then the circuit court—Judge C.M. Thomas and District

Attorney Chaney—approved Neuner's coming onboard as the state's "special assistant district attorney" or "special prosecutor."

The insults were not over for District Attorney Chaney. George Roberts was a prominent Medford attorney who had served as district attorney before returning to a successful private practice (and who later would become president of the Oregon State Bar). Roberts was assigned temporarily to serve as another special prosecutor and as special assistant district attorney. It would be his assignment to assist Neuner, not Chaney. Clearly, Neuner and Roberts were "hired guns" who would prosecute in the Jackson County Circuit Court. To assuage the seemingly demoted Chaney, he would be referred to as the prosecution's "strategist."

As excitement about Hugh's trial began to build, he found opportunity to make good on his promise to be a model prisoner. One Sunday, Sheriff Jennings was at a ballgame, and jailer Ike Dunford also was away. An old officer, Ham Leggitt, had charge of the jail. Upstairs, Bill Jennings, the sheriff's elderly father, was with Hugh, though not in his cell. Two young bootleggers in custody were visiting friends downstairs in the reception room. Seeing that the jail was open, all doors unlocked, one of the boys struck Leggitt, stunning him long enough for the prisoners to scamper out the door. Upstairs, the older Jennings had no weapon and would have been no match had young Hugh wanted to flee. Leggitt recovered and ran out of the jail, shooting at the escapees. A jail trustee shouted out, warning everyone to stop and not leave the area. In the confusion, Leggitt ran back into the jail, waving his pistol. Suddenly, Hugh called down cheerfully, "I'm still here, Ham!" Hugh had opportunity to escape and maybe save his life, but this time, he made a better choice.[6]

TWELVE GOOD MEN AND TRUE

Hugh's trial began with jury selection on May 2, 1927. It was an arduous process. Eager potential jurors had to convince attorneys grilling them that they had no preconceived notions of the defendant's guilt or innocence and had no knowledge of the case (except from minor street corner gossip). Prosecutors looked for jurors who had no objection to hanging a man found guilty. During jury selection, there was much discussion of circumstantial evidence, reasonable doubt and capital punishment. Fortunately, Jackson

County had compiled a list of more than five hundred veniremen (juror candidates). It took until noon of the second day to select the jury:

- *B.M. Bush, electrician, Willow Springs*
- *James E. Clemens, orchardist, Medford*
- *S.W. Dunham, clerk, Medford*
- *C.W. Davis, city employee, Medford*
- *Frank Earhart, farmer, Medford*
- *Fred Fredenburg, teamster, Medford*
- *S.E. Heberling, Central Point*
- *E.N. Judy, retired farmer, Griffin Creek*
- *Nick W. Kime, farmer, Medford*
- *Albert Piche, merchant, Medford*
- *F.W. Wiley, merchant, Central Point*
- *W. Ward, farmer, Eagle Point*[7]

The jury's composition was interesting: no women (several were questioned but rejected), no one from Ashland (home of the murdered mail clerk and brakeman), one slightly deaf, one more deaf, three who chewed tobacco and one who was afraid of firearms. Following jury selection, the state opened its case with a few short remarks from Special Prosecutor George Neuner. Neuner was prominent in the legal community; his title and presence gave weight to the horrific nature of the crime and gravity of the trial. Neuner then handed off to George Roberts, another special prosecutor who would be Neuner's assistant. Roberts was well prepared but needed all morning to present the prosecution's opening statements. The third member of the prosecuting trio was District Attorney Chaney, but it soon became evident that he would speak very little. Appearances and oratory would be handled by the fiery Neuner and his able assistant, Roberts.[8]

This was a contentious trial from the start. Widely publicized, it drew national and international attention. No one could afford to lose. One had to be cautious; Roberts knew that bad things could happen to those connected to the legal profession. As a precaution, he sent his wife and two daughters to visit grandparents in Cincinnati for the duration of the trial.[9]

Hugh sat between his parents but was not very attentive. There was a quiet, nervous energy in the courtroom as Roberts droned on through the state's opening. His carefully structured presentation reminded Hugh of debate classes back at Artesia High School, but the stakes here were far greater.

Roberts summarized that the state would show that Ray and Roy DeAutremont were connected with the crime, but so was a third man. Three sets of creosote-dipped foot pads made from burlap were found together. Human hairs, fabric samples, garments and a towel suggested that the items were used by more than one person. Similarities suggested that two could have been twins. Three tin cups nearby were used by three people. Three men had occupied the camp where the murderers awaited the train, and clearly Hugh was the third man.[10] The state would show, Roberts continued, that remnants of pots, pans, dishes, utensils, an iron buckle from a mackinaw coat and eyelets of a tarpaulin cover were found in a fire pit near the cabin, and all would tie Hugh and two others with him to the crime.

Roberts continued with an audacious "confession" that Hugh was said to have made to Belle as she visited him at Alcatraz prison. Supposedly, she urged him to "make a clean breast of it," and he is said to have replied, "Mother it must have been awful hard for you to know that your nineteen-year-old boy had gone wrong, but I didn't mean to do it." When Belle suggested it would be difficult to come up with an alibi, Hugh allegedly responded, "I know it, but I have a weird story to tell, and with the aid of a good lawyer I can get a jury to believe it."[11] Perhaps there had been ears to the wall during their Alcatraz visit. Now in the courthouse, Hugh looked at Belle in total confusion, as though he'd never heard these words before.

Roberts continued. The Colt Arms Manufacturing Company would show that the hidden serial number on the Colt .45 automatic pistol found near the tracks (no. 130-763) allowed it to be traced from Colt, through Schwabacher Hardware Company of Seattle and Hauser Brothers of Salem and Albany, to "William Elliott," one of Ray's aliases. The DuPont detonator used by the bandits was the one stolen from a construction site near Oregon City. Two deputies investigating the crime scene, Vincent Arcega and L.D. Forncrook, found a pair of bib overalls about half a mile down the track from the west portal. The prosecution would show that these were Roy's. John McCracken of the Park Garage in Ashland would testify that Hugh brought the Nash in for repairs.[12] A cap found near the track looked like one worn by Hugh. Affixed to a black valise found near White Point siding was part of an express tag no. 1723-G that originated in Lakewood, New Mexico. Another portion of the express tag was found in the fire pit at the cabin.

The state would prove that Hugh killed deadheading brakeman Charles "Coyl" Johnson. Johnson, Roberts noted, had rushed forward to aid the enginemen, only to be brutally murdered.

Judge Charles M. Thomas of the Jackson Country Circuit Court presided over the DeAutremont trials. *Southern Oregon Historical Society, #10948.*

In spite of the prosecution's impressive lists of evidence and witnesses, its case was circumstantial and weak. There was only one living witness, express messenger helper Haffey. In the mail car's baggage compartment just before the explosion, he had looked out a side door and saw shadowy figures running through the smoke near the tunnel exit. However, he could not testify that he had seen the defendant Hugh DeAutremont. Unable to tie Hugh directly to the crime, prosecutors would have to wear their best poker faces.

Whereas the prosecution's opening statement took all morning to present, the defense's, presented by Fred Smith, was only three pages long. Brevity, they hoped, would show the confidence that Collier, Newbury and Smith wanted to project: the prosecution has nothing.

With Neuner on the floor, the prosecution called its first witness, Conductor J.O. Marrett, who answered direct questions about what he saw and did just after the tunnel explosion. John Collier cross-examined for the defense. Watching body language and listening, observers got the first hints that there would be hostility between prosecuting and defending attorneys. Throughout the trial, there were terse objections, copious sarcasm and eventually snarls.

One of the most difficult parts of the trial involved exhumation of Brakeman Johnson's body. It was not clear from early investigation how many bandits fired at Johnson and which weapons they used. Former coroner John Perl and Dr. William W. P. Holt painted a gruesome picture. This was necessary, the state argued, to prove that there were distinct wounds from two different weapons and two shooters: one with a shotgun and the other with a pistol. Dr. Holt testified that reexamination of Johnson's wounds just one week before the trial showed that he was on his knees when another shot was fired into his right shoulder, exiting his lower chest.[13] Powerful testimony, this "execution" was an important link in the state's case. The defense was not buying the state's story; Collier challenged the prosecution to put the defendant within a mile of a firearm.

Lawrence E.C. Joers (sometimes misspelled "Jorges"), the young nurse/medical student from Tacoma, Washington, told the packed courtroom what he found, fighting his way through tunnel smoke and gases to the remains of Dougherty and the three trainmen. He and Conductor Marrett were two of the first to reach the locomotive and the "injured" trainmen (would-be rescuers still thought that injuries had resulted from a ruptured boiler). Joers's testimony caused great discomfort in the courtroom. In short, he reported that there were indications that possibly all three trainmen could have been alive, *if very briefly*, when he reached them. He was quick to add that there was no first aid he could have administered to save their lives.[14]

MISTRIAL

S.W. Dunham was a seventy-three-year-old juror from Central Point. Believing that he had stomach flu, he and his doctor thought he could fight it off. However, following an attack in the courtroom on Monday, May 9, the judge called for a recess, and Dunham was taken home to regain his health.

During a light moment, Sheriff Jennings reflected to Hugh that what they needed was an alternate, a thirteenth juror for emergencies like this. Hugh shot back, "For the love of Mike, don't say anything about a 13th juror. That number is unlucky for me. That train was number 13, the tunnel was number 13; now you're talking about a 13th juror, and I'm fighting for my life!"[15]

Mr. Dunham died at home of kidney failure on May 11; Judge Thomas declared a mistrial and scheduled a new trial to begin on June 6. Everyone was shocked by the specter of having to start over. Hugh returned to his cell, quiet and feigning bravado with a weak smile. The novelty gone and the plot predictable, there was less interest in the second trial than the first. It opened with a courtroom only one-third full, not completely filled as during the first trial. Finding twelve satisfactory jurors required interviewing 288 veniremen over four days. Those selected (their professions not readily available) were:

- *R.S. Daniels, Medford*
- *Wm. F. Darby, Ashland*
- *Fred B. Dutton, Medford*
- *Thomas Farlow, Lake Creek*
- *Henry W. Frame, Phoenix*
- *W.W. Hittle, Gold Hill*
- *M.J. Kerney, Central Point*
- *Paul W. Marin, Central Point*
- *Frank Miller, Ashland*
- *L.O. Norcross, Ashland*
- *Earl W. Weaver, Central Point*
- *R.A. Wideman, Eagle Point*[16]

In the meantime, witnesses were recalled from all over the country for a new trial, and the process began again. Worn down by nearly four months of living in a small cell and enduring the monotonous trial routine of opening statements, direct questioning, cross questioning, summations, rebuttals and objections, Hugh grew gaunt and solemn. His manner and facial expressions suggested deep soul-searching and discouragement. He had gone over and over every ploy he could think of; what could he do to avoid the gallows?

Sadly, the distraught widows of Mail Clerk Dougherty and Fireman Seng were called to the witness stand early in the second trial. Adding insult to injury, each had to make arrangements for the small child she had in tow in order to testify.

The parade of evidence and witnesses continued: eighty-six items and seventy-two witnesses.[17] Some had worked with Hugh and the twins in the logging camp near Silverton, where Hugh was known as "E.E. James." Some told of his obsession with the book *The Life of Jesse James* and his practicing marksmanship. They noted that the three boys had left the logging camp together about one month before the crime. George Steffis, a Greek track-walker, testified that a man who looked like Hugh had asked him for a cigarette near the tunnel two days before the crime. Grace Deeter, the postmistress at Deeter, a one-building community near the tunnel, sold supplies to a man who could have been Hugh. A Mexican laborer said that he'd given a cigarette to someone who looked like Hugh the day before the holdup. Workers near the tunnel found iron straps in a cold campfire. Distinctive welding identified the straps as being part of the green trunk with which Hugh had traveled. Pieces of

May 20th, 1927.

Mr. C. Riddiford,
Post Office Inspector in Charge,
Spokane, Washington.

Dear Mr. Riddiford,

I have just had a talk with Judge Thomas about the
DeAutremont case. He and I both want it disposed of
at the earliest possible date, but it seems that the
State is representing that the Government want it
delayed on account of some one or more of your Postal
Inspectors having left for foreign points and that
they cannot be obtained short of about September 1st.
If you could assure me that you are ready to proceed
I believe I could get the Judge to set the trial very
soon. Let me know personally as I am very anxious to
get the responsibility of this prisoner off my hands.
As you know our facilities are entirely inadequate.

With the newspapers making a hero of Hugh I am sure
the State is losing ground each day.

With personal regards, I am,

                              Very truly yours,

                              Ralph G. Jennings
RGJ/o   Sheriff of Jackson County, Oregon

Sheriff Jennings, concerned about trial expenses, warns Riddiford. *Jackson County Archives,*
May 20, 1927.

evidence—circumstantial evidence—came together to tie Hugh closer to the twins and bring them all closer to the scene and time of the crime.

A break in the dour mood of the trial, the defense orchestrated a brief courtroom visit from Hugh's "loving" five-year-old half-brother, Charlie, and ten-year-old stepsister, Inez (both born to Paul's second wife, Nellie). Spying Hugh, the children dashed across the room and showered him with more hugs and kisses than might be expected of kids having little contact with Hugh. But smiles turned back into frowns as Postal Inspector Charles Jefferson took the stand to elaborate on Hugh's supposed "confession" to Belle at Alcatraz. The evidence was suspect but damaging to the defense.[18]

An old miner was one of the last prosecution witnesses. He testified that the day after the murders, he had been out in the brush when a man jumped out and pointed a gun at him. The stranger demanded that the miner show him the way to the Blue Ledge mine. "And hurry!" he added.

"Oh, you're damn right I hurried," assured the miner. Collier, a skilled defense attorney who had made quick work of other witnesses, challenged the miner.

"Are you sure it was the defendant?" The miner wasn't intimidated or hesitant.

"Hell, yes!" The white-bearded geezer jumped from the witness stand, ran to where Hugh was sitting, pointed a damning finger across the railing and declared, "It was this guy! I can tell by the glint in his eye! Did you ever have a guy throw a gun on you?"[19] Collier took his seat for the moment.

Hoping that it was saving the best for last, the state introduced Professor Edward Oscar Heinrich, the chemistry teacher, scientist and "criminologist" from the University of California–Berkeley. Carefully explaining new investigative techniques, Professor Heinrich recounted how he collected and analyzed the wealth of evidence and detailed information involved in this crime. Each item an important piece of the puzzle—there were human hairs, sawdust, pine needles, frayed clothing, fingernail clippings, criminals' descriptions and, of course, the overlooked money order receipt that Heinrich found deep in the bib overalls' pencil pocket.

Mr. Collier and the defense tried to discredit Professor Heinrich's techniques and findings, saying that they relied on "suppositions" and "personal deductions" rather than hard evidence. In fact, Professor Heinrich did offer hard evidence that damaged the defense's case and advanced the study of criminology by years.[20] The defense cross-examined Professor Heinrich, and then the state rested.

Everyone was exhausted. Hugh was stoic, straining to maintain a military bearing. Belle and especially Paul were stressed to the edge of composure. The attorneys' foreheads glistened as they perspired through their arguments. The jurors, sequestered for two weeks, were losing their patience.

Suddenly, the story of the DeAutremont brothers took a turn. On June 8, during Hugh's trial in Jacksonville, officials in Oregon were notified that twins Ray and Roy had been captured in Steubenville, Ohio. This was not good news for Hugh's case. His attorneys' ploy was to portray younger brother Hugh as influenced, dominated and victimized by Ray and Roy. Introducing the twins into the picture now could shift attention and sentiments, make Hugh seem less innocent and jeopardize his defense.

Jackson County sheriff Ralph Jennings and his son, Deputy Sheriff Louis Jennings, set out for Steubenville to take custody of and transport the twins to Oregon. For security and safety, Pullman compartments were arranged for the returning party, which would include Ray and Roy, the sheriff and his deputy, two federal detectives, two postal inspectors and two Ohio detectives. They began their five-day trip to Oregon on June 15 and arrived in Portland on June 20. Union Pacific passenger trains from the east crossed the Willamette River on the Steel Bridge and terminated at Portland's Union Station. This train stopped one mile short at SP's East Morrison Street station, where it would be safer to transfer the prisoners to SP train No. 13 for the overnight trip to Medford. When it arrived at Medford at 10:35 a.m. the next morning, two automobiles waiting beside the station platform met the travelers and whisked them seven miles west to the Jackson County Courthouse. Manacled to the sheriff was Ray, hair lightened by peroxide and having married an Ohio girl and fathered a son. In custody now and torn from family, Ray was a somber, tragic figure. Chained to the deputy was Roy, who tried to manage a little smile and casual bravado. Of the other lawmen who had traveled cross-country with the Jennings/DeAutremont entourage, some left in Portland and others continued to Medford.

At that same time, Hugh was escorted from his cell into the courthouse to hear, hopefully, the last day of the trial and the case turned over to the jury. The cars pulled up, and the twins were taken to the jail's reception room to process in and have their manacles removed. Here, they were able to greet their parents through the bars—the first time they had been together in four years. "Hello, Mama," whispered the twins. Belle wept, and Paul stood quietly. Free of chains now, Ray and Roy were escorted upstairs to Hugh's temporarily vacant cell.

As Sheriff Ralph Jennings escorts his new guests between the jail and courthouse, their expressions give away their feelings. *Robert M. Barker photo, Southern Oregon Historical Society, #14431.*

With the twins settled into a jail cell and the grounds crawling with reporters, this was a good time for a press conference. Authorities hoped to learn something of value if the brothers were allowed to speak freely. It appeared that Roy might take the bait: "If it was under different circumstances, we'd be glad to be back. As it is, it's mighty fine to have Dad and Mother greet us with smiles. The papers practically accused us of the crime, and we knew we'd be lynched if discovered. We were happy, and we hoped and prayed that the real criminals would be caught so we could again live out of the shadow and under our own names."[21] Nothing unexpected there: the boys insisted that they were innocent. Fate willing, they soon would clear their names and live normal, happy lives.

Back on June 17, a few days before the twins arrived in Oregon, the state rested its case against Hugh DeAutremont.[22] In contrast to the state, the defense called only six character witnesses. Three neighbors of the old miner testified that he was an entertaining storyteller but blind as a bat. They had heard his story before of the stranger asking about the Blue Ledge mine. It seemed to change each time he talked about the man with the gun: seven feet tall, very muscular and bewhiskered. The defense noted that Hugh was five-foot-five, only one inch taller than required to join the army.[23]

Another witness was Miss Mary Sands, one of Hugh's teachers at Artesia High School in New Mexico. She offered to testify to Hugh's academic achievements and what she saw as his strong, positive personality traits. Because she was young and attractive, some jumped to the conclusion that theirs was more than an academic relationship. Hugh did not expect Miss Sands to attend the trial, saying, "I'm surprised she believed I was that smart. In fact, I would have guessed just the opposite."[24]

Jack Vick was an army buddy of Hugh's who served with him in Manila. Hugh had lied about Jack being underage to help him enlist. Jack did not make friends easily and was especially grateful when Hugh took him under his wing, treating Jack like the brothers Hugh missed. Out of the army now, Jack rode the rods to get to Jacksonville, and he arrived dirty in tattered clothes. Young news reporter Mary Greiner felt so sorry for Jack that she and friends took him to downtown Medford to buy him clothing. Jack was terrified at the thought of testifying, but he felt better in clean clothes. He felt that he owed his life to best friend Hugh. Irony followed, as years later, Jack died beneath a train as he tried to ride the rods west to visit Hugh in the penitentiary.[25]

A failed alibi attempt showed the support of friends for the beleaguered family. Paul and his family had an elderly friend in Eugene, Mrs. Lydia Morton, landlady of a sizeable boardinghouse on Seventh Avenue. Mrs. Morton must have been a dear friend to take the stand and testify that her guest register showed Hugh staying in the boardinghouse. However, it was at a time he was meeting with the Ashland mechanic, trying to speed up repairs to the Nash. Mrs. Morton could not explain the discrepancy and so lost credibility. Knowing that Hugh had stayed at her rooming house helps understand the boys' habits. Although they occasionally called Paul's Eugene house "home," his family-by-marriage was too large to take visitors into his tiny bungalow (wife, a preschooler, two young twins, a nephew and a tenant). It was Mrs. Morton's boardinghouse that gave the brothers a place to stay in Eugene whenever they needed it.[26]

Although exhausted by the emotion and monotony of the trials, Belle took the stand as the final defense witness to swear that Hugh had *not* said to her at Alcatraz, "I didn't mean to go wrong."

The defense rested after only half a day of testimony. Surprisingly, his lawyers did not put Hugh on the stand or offer other alibis. They felt that changing sentiment was a more important tool. In some public circles, the

Mary K. Sands (middle photo), a teacher at Artesia New Mexico high school, was one of few character witnesses called by the defense. *Robert J. Bruce and Southern Oregon Historical Society, PAM#373 A6.*

146

Mr. F. C. Adams, Principal
University of Colorado,
Boulder, Colo.

Miss Jean McCaleb
Latin and History
University of Arkansas,
Batesville, Ark.

Mrs. Mabel Iler
Commercial
Barnes Commercial College
Denver, Colo.

Miss Esther La Due
English and Spanish
Greenville College,
Greenville, Ill.

Mr. H. Davis
Mathematics and Science
Simmons College,
Abilene, Texas

Miss Mary K. Sands
English
University of New Mexico
Albuquerque, New Mexico

Mr. Ralph Reed
*Manual Training and
Industrial Arts*
Kansas State Normal
Hays, Kansas

Mr. O. K. Evans
Mathematics and Science
William Jewell College
Liberty, Mo.

Miss Ruth Ann Morgan
Domestic Science and Art
Kansas A. & M. College,
Manhattan, Kansas

Paul DeAutremont, distraught father of the three Tunnel 13 criminals, pauses in the courtyard during a break in Hugh's trial. *Southern Oregon Historical Society, #2287.*

clamor to hang Hugh had softened considerably since 1923. In the words of Medford resident Ruth Schleigh, whose family lived across the street from the Jackson County jail and who watched activities during the trials as a fourteen-year-old schoolgirl, "There was such a crowd. We'd see [Hugh] going between buildings. He was just so cute!"[27]

Newton Chaney was basically silent during the trial; Roberts delivered the state's case.[28] With powerful oratory, Roberts sought to repair gaps where evidence was circumstantial (as most was). He hammered on Hugh's supposed "confession" to his mother, and he painted the young Hugh as a coldblooded fiend who didn't hesitate to execute Coyl Johnson.

When Roberts finished, John Collier pleaded for the defense. How could we be sure, he challenged, that Hugh committed murder? There were no eyewitnesses. Collier suggested that the murders could have been an inside job. After all, he claimed, these trainmen had "scabbed" (continued working after a strike had led co-workers to walk off the job). He noted that railroad vengeance can be brutal at times.[29] Hugh, he argued, was an accomplished, respected youth who had never been in any trouble. How, Collier asked, could he turn from being a model youth into a killer: a cool, plotting deliberate butcher of human beings?

June 21 was the day of final arguments, and Gus Newbury began for the defense. The temperature was in the eighties, and everyone was tired and uncomfortable. Straining to defend the innocence of a young boy, there was more emotion and sarcasm in Newbury's voice than normal. This was not wasted on the prosecution, and attorneys' neck hairs began to bristle. Sarcasm turned to contempt as Newbury concluded his defense plea.

Now the state's turn for summation, Neuner could not wait a second longer. He jumped to the floor like a rabid animal. As he stormed back and forth in front of the jurors, his manner intimidated everyone. It probably was not the best time for Roy, next door in a cell, to begin singing his heart out in futile protest to the DeAutremonts' condition in life: "You'll never miss your mother till she's gone."

As if rebutting, Neuner could be heard roaring, "And justice can only be met if this cold-blooded killer, this willing slayer of innocent men, this human buzzard who gloried in the death-struggles of his helpless victims, is hanged by his neck until his miserable life is ended."

Roy sang louder, trying to drown out Neuner's condemnation of his younger brother: "Oh Daddy, don't work in the mines today, for dreams so often come true." Sobbing sometimes accompanied Roy's high notes. Ray stood silently.[30]

Suddenly, Neuner turned his wrath away from the defendant and toward Collier. "Why did you insult the deductive conclusions of Professor Heinrich?" Catching Collier off-guard and speechless, Neuner shifted his diatribe to Gus Newbury. Newbury dismissed him, saying, "Talk to the jury, not to me."

JUDGE THOMAS'S INSTRUCTIONS TO JURORS

From the Medford Mail Tribune, June 20, 1927.

"Instructions of Court Give Five Verdicts"

Judge Thomas Outlines Jury's Duties as Trial of Hugh DeAutremont Ends—Caution Urged Regarding Expert Testimony.

Courthouse, Jacksonville, Ore, June 21—(AP)—The court in its instructions to the jury in the Hugh DeAutremont trial today at 2:30 p.m. left five choices of verdict possible, as follows:

Guilty of murder in the first degree as charged in the indictment, which will carry with it the death penalty.

Guilty of murder in the first degree as charged in the indictment, but recommendation of life imprisonment in lieu of the death penalty.

Guilty of murder in the second degree.

Guilty of manslaughter.

Verdict of not guilty.

There were 28 articles in the instructions summarized as follows:

Jury should not consider remarks of court or counsel during hearing of evidence or use against the defendant the fact that an indictment has been returned against him, as it is a legal form.

The jury should not consider the ruling of the court as evidence; the presumption of innocence rests with the defendant and he must have benefit of any reasonable doubt.

First and second degree murder, manslaughter, conspiracy, circumstantial evidence and motive were all legally defined by the court.

Flight, said the court, is to be considered as legally defined and is not sufficient in itself to establish guilt, but must be used as circumstance. An alibi is a legal form of evidence. It is not incumbent to establish it beyond a reasonable doubt.

Expert testimony was then defined, and the court closed as follow: "All that has been said in regard to experts and expert testimony is subject to the rule that all testimony of experts must be received and weighed with great caution."

This scene in the courtyard during a break in Hugh's trial captures interesting characters. *Southern Oregon Historical Society, #2222.*

Furious, Neuner snarled, "I'll talk to you any time I feel like it." Both attorneys took steps forward, and Newbury began to pull off his coat while growling, "I'll talk to you outside."[31]

Had it not been for Judge Thomas pounding his gavel frantically and observers ready to intervene, a fistfight probably would have ensued. If attorneys have reputations for leaving contention behind and sharing libations after heated trials, that camaraderie would not have occurred here. With civility somewhat restored, Neuner apologized to the court superficially and completed the state's summation. Newbury offered the final defense plea, and Neuner rebutted it. The trial came to a close.

That afternoon at 4:30 p.m. (2:30 p.m., according to the aforementioned article), on June 21, 1927, Hugh's case went to the jury. Five minutes later, Ray and Roy were led into the courtroom for arraignment. They passed Hugh in the dark, silent hallway, but no one spoke, even though the twins had not seen Hugh for three and a half years. A painfully long, tedious process began: the county clerk, Delila Stevens, read four indictments against each twin: one for the murder of each trainman and one for the mail clerk. To each charge, the response was not guilty.[32]

Elderly bailiff George Lewis nearly ran from the jury room to the courtroom: the jury had reached its verdict—in only one hour and forty-five minutes. The twins were hustled from their arraignment back to the jail cell while Hugh was returned to the courtroom for the verdict. Again the brothers passed in the hallway, and again they did not speak.[33] Critical choices had just been made: innocent or guilty, life or death. Hugh sat near his parents, every muscle in his body tensed.

Things began happening quickly. The jury's decision was guilty of first-degree murder as charged, but the sentence, read with the verdict, was life in prison, not the dreaded death by hanging. The press erupted into a shouting match, wanting to know if the defense would appeal. Of course they would appeal, Smith answered; no one liked the way Judge Thomas had handled the trial, he said. Their reactions seemed somewhat different in private. Smith and Collier said that they were satisfied with the outcome. Newbury wept; he was sure that he had been defending an innocent boy.[34]

What had just happened was reasonable. A horrible, heinous crime had been committed, and Hugh had a role in it. But the evidence against him was circumstantial; there were no eyewitnesses who saw Hugh. The jury did not feel that the state had put the gun that killed Johnson into Hugh's hand, and without direct evidence, it could not hang him.

Suddenly, things were hopping, and people were bumping into one another in the courthouse halls. Almost immediately, there began a series of off-the-record meetings between District Attorney Chaney, Sheriff Jennings, defense attorneys and the twins. With circumstantial evidence issues and the specter of appeal hanging overhead, Chaney and the county wanted to be done with the DeAutremonts and get them out of town.

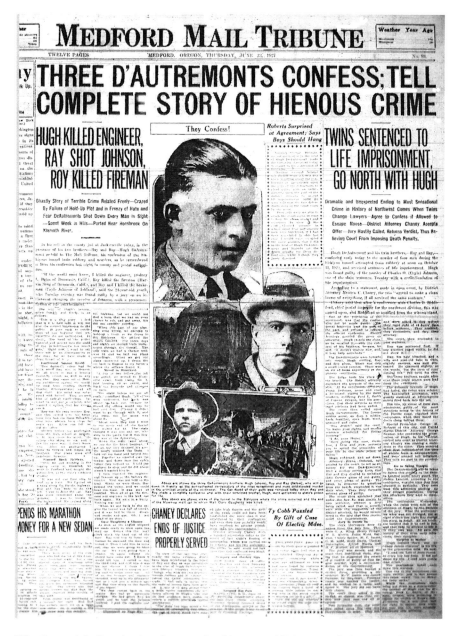

Wheeling and dealing, the three boys confess. Neuner and Roberts are furious. *From the* Medford Mail Tribune, *June 23, 1927.*

An appeal trial for Hugh, two more trials for the twins, then appeals for them would be very expensive and time-consuming. Even worse would have been an appeal leading to an acquittal, and with the evidence issues, that was possible. Although the sheriff no longer feared a lynch mob, he was growing more worried about the tremendous costs of caring for his three guests.

That evening, with Chaney and Jennings doing most of the talking, the twins were offered a deal close to what Hugh ended up with: life imprisonment with no death penalty in exchange for signed confessions, no possibility of parole and no lessening of indictments. There was very little hesitation because the twins wanted to live. Chaney and Jennings made it clear that evidence against the twins was overwhelming, so they could not take their chances with a jury trial, as Hugh had, and expect to live. Hugh was lucky; the twins probably would not be.[35]

On June 22, bargaining for an outcome like Hugh's, Ray and Roy announced that they were willing to change their pleas to "guilty" and confess to their roles in the crimes. Hugh then voluntarily confessed, hoping that would help the twins.[36] By agreement between the court and the defense, the DeAutremonts' one condition in confessing was that Roy be allowed to give a long, unrestricted confession for all three. The others would be present to offer corrections. An assistant district attorney, George Neilson, took all three confessions in shorthand, a huge task. Transcribed, Roy's confession was forty-two legal-size pages long. The other boys' confessions were only a few pages. It is no surprise that Roy's confession blamed economic conditions, dysfunctional family and even heredity for their crime and demise. Neilson began taking dictation at 8:00 p.m. on June 22 and finished the documents at 6:00 a.m. the next morning.

A complication arose. Two days earlier, the twins had hired Fred Smith, from Hugh's defense team. Now they did not want Smith; they told Sheriff Jennings that they wanted Frank DeSouza to represent them. DeSouza rushed to the courthouse. He met with Chaney and agreed on the deal that would avoid the death penalty. Everything seemed ready for signatures when another issue, one more complicated, surfaced: Judge Thomas was not empowered to sentence the twins to life. In fact, on a confession with no jury trial, he would be compelled by law to sentence the twins to the gallows. Avoiding this would require a jury trial—the third for the DeAutremonts. The clerk drew twelve names from the jury box, and the court quickly impaneled a jury, all members from Medford:

- *Scott Davis*
- *Thomas Dunnington*
- *W.F. Isaacs*
- *C.M. Kidds*
- *H.F. Meador*
- *W.E. Morris*
- *Alfred Norris*
- *Henry Pringle*
- *Claude Saylor*
- *C.A. Wing*
- *Jonas Wold*
- *(Mr.) Barnum*[37]

With the jury seated, the boys' freshly signed confessions were read, and Judge Thomas issued his instructions to the jury. Noting the circumstances of Hugh's crime and trial, the judge expected the same verdict and penalty for the twins. Jury Foreman Isaacs signed and returned the verdict to the judge: first-degree murder with recommendation of life imprisonment.[38]

At a press conference, Hugh showed his old spirit, "When the eternal potter molded the DeAutremont boys, he might have slipped a little, but he only poured in too much guts."[39]

One reporter who had opportunity to observe Hugh and Roy together at Jacksonville remarked later, "There was no remorse in their voices as they joyously, like schoolboys describing an adventure, recounted the murders."[40] Certainly there were smiles on their faces—they just beat the death penalty.

Noticeably, Ray did not share his brothers' jocularity or enjoy banter with the press. His attitude was more philosophical: "Mercy has done more for us than anything

As a special prosecutor, George Roberts should have been party to any negotiating in the circuit court. *U.S. Post Office Department.*

155

else. We all see now that murder is a terrible thing, and we couldn't before. I've been pessimistic, I'll confess, but I've been transformed. I've learned that every evil has a brighter side, and from now on I'm going to be optimistic."[41]

SETTLING IN

The DeAutremont brothers had worn out their welcome in Jacksonville. There was another reaction to the court's leniency: in Ashland, angry citizens hanged and burned the DeAutremonts in effigy. On June 24, 1927, the three brothers were transported by an SP passenger train to their new home, the Oregon State Penitentiary. During the trip, Hugh and Roy were their old selves, smiling and waving at those who knew the murderers to be aboard the train. At one point, Hugh commented, "I think Oregon is a great state. I think I will settle down here."[42]

Those who had worked hardest to find and punish the DeAutremonts were Chief Postal Inspector Riddiford and SP chief special agent O'Connell. No one felt the exhilaration of victory as did Riddiford—he accompanied the

Roberts Surprised at Agreement; Says Boys Should Hang

Attorney George Roberts, special prosecutor in the trial of Hugh DeAutremont, made the following statement today in regard to the confession of the twins.

"Neither George Neuner nor myself were advised nor knew anything about the confessions or agreements upon the part of the defendants to plead guilty with an understanding upon the part of the district attorney to accept life imprisonment, until we were told that the two defendants were in the court room by the press.

"Then only were we able to reach the court room in time to hear the pleas verdict and sentences. In view of the cold blooded manner in which these four unfortunate men were butchered. If I had been associated in this last case I would have occupied the same position that I did in the trial of Hugh DeAutremont and insisted on the death penalty for those defendants, which I think they justly deserved.

Roberts and Neuner were not pleased with Chaney's secret dealings to avoid death penalties. *From the* Medford Mail Tribune, *June 23, 1927.*

boys to the gates of the penitentiary to make sure that they would be safely locked up. O'Connell also felt the victory, but his dogged determination caught up with him: he exhausted himself with the chase and entered a hot springs rest facility, where he followed the trial in the papers.

There were bad feelings between lawyers that would not soon go away. Special Prosecutors Neuner and Roberts claimed that they were left in the dark regarding any negotiating or deal-making. Both adamantly supported the death penalty for the DeAutremonts and insisted that any sentence less than death would be travesty. They claimed that had they not walked by the courthouse pressroom and heard reporters talking, they would not have known about the lifesaving deal between Chaney and the defense. When challenged for his surreptitious deal-making, Chaney cheerfully responded that justice had been served while saving taxpayers the considerable expense of further trials.[13]

Chapter 7

CONFINEMENT

I'll stake my integrity on the fact that they never would repeat a criminal life like
that again.
—Professor Edward O. Heinrich, criminologist

Through the Bars

Ray, Roy and Hugh DeAutremont arrived at their new home, the Oregon State Penitentiary in Salem, on June 24, 1927. A provision of the plea agreement that kept the boys off the gallows stipulated that they would never be eligible for parole.[1] If there was any chance of that changing, it would be decades away. As they entered the "Big House," Roy and Hugh were not thinking about parole—they had just beaten the death penalty. Ray, brokenhearted, still grieved for the family he had left behind in Ohio.

After only a few days, the brothers began to settle into prison life. The twins were allowed to share a cell. The three were assigned to work in the prison's flax mill, and with physical activity, Ray began to come out of his deep depression. On his own time, he returned to the voracious reading of past years. He became a serious student of philosophy, sociology, mathematics, astronomy, Spanish and French. In conversation, he would quote classical thinkers and renowned authors. He contemplated what he called the "forces of cosmic development" and how he got where he was. He argued that, had fate allowed a few things to happen a little differently, the DeAutremonts could have enjoyed very different lives.[2]

Considering their educations, Hugh had been the student, Roy not so much (although interested in religion) and Ray not at all. Now Hugh, living up to his promise to be the model prisoner, sought a meaningful trade for a life career. After a stint in the prison lime plant, Hugh transferred to the laundry, where he worked until 1933. At that time, he moved to the print shop and became interested in all facets of publication.

Hugh took classes in English and writing offered by the University of Oregon and became editor of the defunct prison magazine, *Shadows*. With help from contributing writers like Ray, *Shadows* became an award-winning publication. Hugh and his staff began printing the *Oregon Pulse*, and the print shop stayed busy doing jobs for several state agencies.[3] Hugh was a pleasant, hardworking fellow, and people liked him. State office managers joked that, for the money the print shop was saving, the state never could afford to parole him. In spare time during the 1940s and '50s, Hugh and his print shop crew produced and sold lines of greeting cards. In a letter to family friend Mary E. Smith, Hugh discussed her becoming a commission saleswoman for his lines of cards.[1]

Roy's transition was not stellar. With his eyes giving him less trouble than in the past, he returned to what he knew, becoming a prison barber. But as years went by, Roy showed personality quirks that began to concern officials and his cellmate, Ray. He became confrontational and quarrelsome. More and more, he withdrew into himself. He neglected personal hygiene and began disrespecting authority. During a violent rampage in 1949, six prison guards were required to subdue Roy—hard to believe for his slight stature and forty-nine years. As a boy, he had complained that he was too puny to accomplish much physical labor. But in this episode, he destroyed most of his cell's fixtures and furniture before guards overpowered him.

Fearing danger to Ray and others, prison officials transferred Roy to the Oregon State Mental Hospital. He was diagnosed with schizophrenia and received a prefrontal lobotomy in 1950. Not completely successful, the controversial procedure calmed down Roy, but it also put him into a near-vegetative state for the rest of his life.[5] Again, there is the irony that Roy once worked as a staff attendant in this same hospital. He came to Oregon in 1920 to be closer to his twin during Ray's one-year reformatory term.

No one wants to live in a cage, and it was just a matter of time until the brothers would begin thinking about parole and freedom. Of course,

Above: Oregon State Penitentiary in Salem. *U.S. Post Office Department.*

Opposite, top: On June 24, 1927, the three DeAutremont brothers were transferred to the Oregon State Penitentiary in Salem. Their new identifications became #9903 (Ray, seen here), #9904 (Roy) and #9902 (Hugh). *U.S. Post Office Department.*

Opposite, middle: Roy (#9904). *U.S. Post Office Department.*

Opposite, bottom: Hugh (#9902). *U.S. Post Office Department.*

schizophrenic Roy was not suitable for freedom and would not be seriously considered. Hugh, on the other hand, had become well known for his exemplary behavior and contributions. Many officials, including at least one prison psychiatrist, argued that Hugh was an excellent candidate for parole.[6] Why, then, was such an outstanding prisoner with rehabilitation prospects so great still behind bars? Mainly because of the "no parole" deal in 1927. It threatened, in part, that should anyone explore the idea of parole for Hugh, he could be tried for three remaining circuit court murder indictments—those of the mail clerk and two other trainmen.

There were many whose hatred of the coldblooded killers had not waned—railroad and postal communities, widows and orphans and

SPOKANE DIVISION

Alaska
Idaho
Montana
Oregon
Washington

C. Riddiford

Inspector in Charge
R-J

Post Office Department

OFFICE OF THE INSPECTOR IN CHARGE   CASE No.

SPOKANE, WASH., June 11, 1928.

Chief Inspector:

When Roy and Ray DeAutremont were arrested there were taken from them two old Luger Revolvers. These were sent into the Department. I have an impression that, perhaps, Inspector C. W. B. Long, got one of them and that there still may be one of them in your office.

Mr. Ralph Jennings, Sheriff of Jackson County, Oregon, at Medford, Oregon, did some excellent work on the DeAutremont case, and, if possible he would like one of the revolvers referred to. If such action is not contrary to the policy of the Department I should appreciate it very much if you can see your way clear to send me one of the guns to give to Mr. Jennings. I think he would regard it as a very kindly appreciation of the work done on the case by him.

Inspector in Charge.

cc
Mr. Ralph Jennings,
Medford, Oregon.

"To the victor belong the spoils." We do not know if Sheriff Jennings received his souvenir Luger, but for a man of his influence, it is likely that he did. *Jackson County Circuit Court Archives.*

those immersed in the investigation, search and trial. Officials of the Southern Pacific Railroad and U.S. Post Office Department visited the penitentiary periodically just to make sure that the DeAutremonts had not been released through further deal-making. When a parole hearing for Hugh was scheduled for September 1950, George Neuner, who had been a special prosecutor during the trial, and Jackson County district attorney George Neilson vigorously opposed any consideration of parole. Neuner said, "I will oppose any application for parole of these brothers as long as

I live…I consider the crime in which these brothers were involved among the most serious in the criminal annals of this state." Mr. Neilson agreed, saying, "As long as I am District Attorney, the three indictments will be prosecuted if Hugh DeAutremont should be released."[7]

But there were those who argued just as vehemently that Hugh was not a natural criminal or a threat to society. Perhaps, they said, he was a victim of circumstances, an unfortunate misalignment of Ray's "forces of cosmic development." No fool, Hugh realized that he could garner support by suggesting that he was just going along with what the older twins wanted him to do. In a conversation with Mary Greiner Kelly, Hugh lamented, "Mary, you aren't eighteen years old all your life and you're not always under the domination of two older brothers."[8]

The Kellys

Mary Greiner was just days from receiving her journalism degree from the University of Washington when family friend Dan Bowerman, city editor of the *Medford Daily News*, telephoned and asked her to come to work for his family's newspaper. With Hugh DeAutremont just arrested in the Philippines and bound for Jacksonville, Dan was in the middle of a drama and needed help. Mary felt special when he asked her to cover the crime story. Not only was she a new cub reporter, but she was also the only female in the throng of older, experienced journalists from all over the country. As was the custom, reporters (including editor Bowerman) covered the trial "by day" for their paper and then on their own time cranked out and sold DeAutremont stories as fast as they could write. To quote her during an interview, "'I felt terribly privileged to be with all those seasoned reporters,' she says. They gave her confidence. 'They were very nice to me and they liked the way I wrote…It was a very exciting time. The whole town was on its ear. The air was just charged.'"

A skilled, compassionate listener, Mary may have had advantages that helped her gain interviews with Hugh. She understood the many facets of the trial, including shifting sentiments. She remarked, "Hugh had a boyish face and curly, light hair. He looked so young, people had a lot of sympathy for him." More importantly, "The evidence against the DeAutremonts was circumstantial. That's what gave Hugh a break in sympathy."[9]

With all its complexity and drama, the DeAutremont story had a life of its own. Some of the relationships that formed were unexpected and quite interesting. SP chief special agent Dan O'Connell visited the brothers in prison to make sure that they still were there. Over time, he grew somewhat cordial toward the boys and seemed to enjoy banter with them. One of the brothers was heard to ask, "Hey Dan, how about that pardon?" O'Connell didn't mind a little humor, but all knew that he was steadfastly against paroles for these coldblooded killers.[10]

Also unlikely was the friendship that formed between Mary Greiner, friend of Hugh and Belle DeAutremont, and Professor Edward O. Heinrich, criminal investigator and primary witness for the prosecution. Mary interviewed and corresponded many times with Heinrich over the years. Regarding Hugh, Heinrich told her that he'd stake his professional reputation on this being a "one-time-only" crime.[11]

In August 1929, Mary wed Medford attorney Edward C. Kelly. By this time, she had left the *Medford Daily News* and was reporting for the *Medford Mail Tribune*. Edward served in the Oregon legislature during the early 1930s, and then he and Mary moved to Washington, D.C., where he served as an assistant U.S. attorney during the New Deal era. They returned to Oregon in the 1930s, and Edward worked for the Bonneville Power Administration in Portland. Moving home to Medford during World War II, Edward went off to war, and Mary, in spite of their growing family, became very involved in national, state and local Democratic Party activities (politics would become a lifelong passion for her). Edward returned from the military and began his own law practice in Medford. He was appointed circuit court judge in 1957.

Very involved in civics and causes, Mary stayed in touch with the DeAutremont family, especially Hugh. With her husband an attorney and then a judge, she had legal advice and Edward's support in her tireless efforts to free Hugh. The following letter from Mary to the parole board in 1948 is offered in its entirety because it accurately portrays changing public sentiments and the Kelly family's efforts to free Hugh:

LETTER TO THE PAROLE BOARD ON HUGH DEAUTREMONT, PRISONER #9902, DATED NOVEMBER 16, 1948

From: Mrs. Edward C. Kelly
906 West Fourth Street
Medford, Oregon

This is to respectfully ask your consideration of a parole for Hugh D'Autremont, who has now served twenty-one years of a life sentence in the state penitentiary, for his part in the Siskiyou tunnel murder of 1923. It is my understanding that under a recently enacted law, it is possible, upon good behavior, to be eligible for a parole after eight years of such a sentence has been served.

The Oregon constitution specifically provides that the object of imprisonment shall be reformation not punishment. The devotion of enlightened boards of parole and probation to rehabilitation and reformation, plus the plain mandate of the Oregon constitution which they are sworn to uphold, seems to call for careful consideration of this particular case. Otherwise, after 21 years of imprisonment, what incentive is there left, if a man, who has worked as zealously as Hugh D'Autremont, to prove himself, couldn't be given consideration for parole?

It is my information, that during the more than two decades he has served, there has never been any inmate with a higher record for behavior and performance. As editor of the prison publication, Shadows, and more recently, in complete charge of the institution's printing, he has proved himself capable of taking responsibility, guiding and directing others, and turning his talents to worthwhile account. In a recent interview with him he expressed particular pride and gratification that he and his staff had handled the printing for so many charitable and philanthropic drives such as the Tubercular Seal Sales, children's homes and schools, etc. This indicates, I feel, a right attitude toward community responsibility.

As a newspaper reporter I covered the D'Autremont trial in 1927, have made my home in the community ever since, and am perhaps as well acquainted as anyone, not only with the complete background and circumstances, but with all the personalities involved in the case. While the D'Autremont case, because of the wide publicity, stands out in the public mind, still this, in itself should not be a factor in withholding just recognition for such a long period of exceptionally good behavior. Also, in the background of the crime itself, were circumstances, I feel, should be taken into consideration by the parole board in reviewing the case of Hugh D'Autremont.

The D'Autremont boys (there were five of them altogether) were the victims of a broken home, the father, after much restless moving around the country, having left the mother to battle it out alone in the God-forsaken desert town of Lakewood, New Mexico. There she did her best to make a home and eke out a living for her five, by running a little general merchandise store.

Dissatisfied, the two oldest boys, the twins, Ray and Roy [actually, Verne was the oldest], *finally followed their father up north into Oregon, seeking work. They found the father had remarried and had inherited a ready-made family of small children to support, so there was no home for them. This, coupled with their inability to find work over a considerable period of time, embittered Ray particularly, and he became obsessed with some erratic, socialistic thinking. He was extremely persuasive and gradually talked his brother Roy into the notion that the world owed them a living, even if they had to violate some laws to get it.*

Opposite: Mary Greiner Kelly, cub reporter during the DeAutremont trial, important civic personality, political activist, wife of Judge Edward Kelly and outstanding journalist. *Oregon Historical Society*.

Left: Mary Greiner Kelly, 1981. *From the* Medford Mail Tribune, *October 29, 1981*.

It was at this time that the two of them came back and got Hugh, then just 18 and out of high school, and took him north with them to "look for work." From then on, he was definitely under the influence and domination of his two older brothers (four years his senior) until after that nightmare of a crime had been committed.

The subject's extreme youth at the time, coupled with his record of fine behavior on all other occasions isolated from this one incident, certainly indicates that he is inherently a good and sound individual. Even following

*the crime, he served two years in the United States Army in the Philippines
making a good record and receiving a promotion.*

*Because of his long period of punishment, his excellent institutional
record, the concrete proof of his reformation and right attitude, and because
he is equipped by training and intelligence to take his place in society, I ask
your board to give this prisoner your just consideration for parole.*[12]

Mary's letter did not gain parole for Hugh, but it helped. As time passed,
opposition softened, and public sentiment continued to shift in his favor.
The crime's chief investigators, Dan O'Connell of the SP and Charles
Riddiford of the U.S. Post Office Department, had been unrelenting in their
pursuit of the DeAutremonts. They vowed to see the brothers die in prison.
But Riddiford died in January 1931 and O'Connell in January 1948. The
two most vehement "DeAutre-phobes" were gone, and every year, the tiny,
graying Hugh looked less like a criminal.

This is not to say that there was great forgiveness. Folks in southern
Oregon would scorn the name "DeAutremont" for years to come. Paul
and his second wife had another son, Charles, born in 1921 and a half-
brother of the older boys. Charlie (also known by friends as "Chuck" in later
years) grew up to be an outstanding student, athlete, coach and educator
in Oregon—as fine a person as any. The author's father played high school
basketball against Chuck's team and could remember spectators booing as
Chuck took the court.

LEGALITIES AND PAROLE

After being apprehended, Hugh was indicted on four counts of first-
degree murder and two lesser charges of interfering with a mail train.
Again, he also was charged in the U.S. Court with two federal counts of
interfering with a mail train, but the court quietly sealed and filed these
away for possible future use, like blocking a parole.[13] He pleaded not
guilty to all charges. He was tried on one murder charge (Coyl Johnson's
death) and was found guilty but was sentenced to life in prison, avoiding
the death penalty.[14] The next day, Ray and Roy confessed, and so did
Hugh. He did not, however, change his plea to guilty on any of the
five remaining indictments. They remained "pending" with a plea of

not guilty for thirty years from 1927 until 1957. Hugh's attorney at the time, Edward Kelly, filed a motion in 1957 to dismiss all five pending indictments. The basis for this was an Oregon statute enacted during the 1950s that guaranteed a defendant the right to a speedy trial. It provided that, if a motion to dismiss were filed in the Oregon Circuit Court, then the court had to set a trial date not more than ninety days later or the indictment would be dismissed.

When Mr. Kelly was appointed a circuit court judge in 1957, his daughter, Noreen, a recent graduate of the University of Oregon Law School, took over Hugh's case. As though welcoming her to a legal foray, Judge H.K. Hanna denied the motion for dismissal. Miss Kelly appealed to the Oregon Supreme Court. The high court denied the dismissal motion, agreeing with Judge Hanna that Hugh waived his right to a speedy trial by "consenting" that the five outstanding indictments be held in abeyance for all those years. Hugh's consent was based on weak "evidence": a hearsay affidavit from an ex-employee of the Post Office. Hugh denied consenting, the court upheld the lower court's decision and now the five outstanding indictments were sent down for Judge Hanna to hear in the Jackson County Circuit Court.

Noreen entered into intense negotiation with Jackson County district attorney Tom Reeder.[15] Her objective was to "clear the deck" of pending indictments so the parole board couldn't keep using its threat as excuses for not paroling Hugh. What would eventually come out of negotiation was agreement that (a) Hugh would now plead guilty to one count of second-degree murder (carrying a penalty of life in prison and thereby avoiding the death penalty); (b) the two remaining murder indictments would be dismissed; (c) the penalty for this new plea would be served *consecutively* with the first penalty; (d) Hugh would plead guilty to either robbery from a mail train or burglary of a mail train, and the other of these two charges would be dismissed; and (e) the penalty for the mail train plea would be served *concurrently*. Part of a different case was a ruling that since a person has only one life, a life verdict "on top" of another life verdict (i.e., consecutive sentences) was a legal nullity. Parties were bound by this ruling, so it removed the consecutive life sentence. Regarding the other indictment (mail train robbery or burglary), it was further agreed to word it so that the sentence would apply *retroactively*. That meant it already had been served.

Hugh's plea of guilty to one second-degree murder charge cleared the two remaining murder indictments, but there were still mail train federal charges with which to contend. Noreen did not know exactly what they would be because the U.S. District Court had ordered the federal indictments sealed back in 1927 (probably at Neuner's insistence that doing so was in the "public good"). The sealed federal indictments were like an insurance policy for those fighting to keep Hugh in prison. Should Hugh be paroled with federal charges unresolved, he could be quickly rearrested and tried on whatever the federal charges might be. This fostered an attitude in the parole board of, "Why should we parole him? He will just be rearrested and tried on federal charges." So, if federal charges were not accessed and dealt with now, they could ruin chances of a parole later.

Noreen went to Portland and recruited the help of federal judge Gus Solomon, who ordered the file opened and the federal indictments made known. As they read, the charges were no more serious than mail train robbery or burglary. There were no murder charges in the federal indictments because there was no provision at the time of the crime for a federal penalty of death in the robbery or burglary of a mail train.[16] Legislation providing for such a death penalty was passed just after the DeAutremont case, but it had not been available to federal prosecutors when the brothers were indicted.

Knowing now exactly how the federal charges read, Noreen tackled those indictments as the next step toward parole. Since the federal court would have to deal with the federal indictments, Noreen and Hugh had to decide whether to ask for a jury trial or plead guilty and throw Hugh to the mercy of Judge Solomon. Nathan Leopold had just written his book *Life Plus 99 Years*, which offered strong argument for rehabilitation and was widely studied and discussed—including by Judge Solomon. There was strong sentiment in the Portland area for Hugh's parole, and even the penitentiary warden supported his release. Hugh and Noreen decided to take their chances with Judge Solomon, and the gamble paid off. Solomon accepted Hugh's federal guilty pleas and commuted the federal sentences to time served on the state charges. The path to Hugh's parole was open now. Sympathy increasingly supported Hugh, and the parole board had run out of excuses.[17] As Noreen McGraw said recently, "The issue at that point was not guilt or innocence but rehabilitation. The path had been charted."[18]

Paroled in 1958, Hugh asked Noreen to represent Ray in his seeking parole. Their process was similar to that used to parole Hugh. Facing strong public sentiment now, Governor Tom McCall commuted any state sentences against Ray. It was still up to the board to grant parole, but with roadblocks removed, the board approved Ray's application.[19] Hugh and Ray were "free," but at what costs?

Chapter 8

MILEPOSTS

Hugh

January 9, 1959, was a typically gray, wet winter day in Salem. Hugh, however, would be the last to call the day gloomy. "Little Hughie," as prisoners respectfully called him, was spending his last few hours behind the thick concrete walls of the Oregon State Penitentiary. He had been paroled. Before the day was over, he would be with his fiancée, the patient, devoted lady whom he met in 1947 while working in the prison print shop. On this day, a big black car pulled up to the prison's main gate. At age fifty-four, Hugh was being given the chance to start over in life.

Those who came together to help launch his new life had secured a job for him as a linotype operator at a newspaper in San Francisco. They also helped him find a small rental room. Hugh and his fiancée were eager to marry, but Hugh felt that he owed it to her to be secure in a job and have his feet firmly on the ground before taking on the responsibilities of marriage. Relocating to San Francisco would help him blend into a large population and be less obvious to those who still had bad feelings for the DeAutremonts.

Under the rules and supervision of the California parole system, ex-convict Hugh was required to delay his marriage for sixty days. He was quietly bitter about this restriction but wanted to do everything just right. His parole officer hoped that the delay would be long enough to adjust to life on the outside.[1]

His job at the newspaper required joining the union, which had a thirty-day residency requirement. The union business agent sensed that something was funny and felt it was his responsibility to clear it up. Why, he asked, had someone with Hugh's many years of printing experience not joined the union before now? Hugh nodded at the paperwork on the agent's desk and shot back, "Take a look at my name!" Surprised and embarrassed, the agent's tone changed, and Hugh was welcomed into the union.[2]

Hugh had worked only six days when a sharp pain sent him to the Veterans' Hospital in San Francisco. After quick exploratory surgery, the doctor explained that Hugh was suffering from lung cancer that could not be treated effectively.[3] Hugh's fiancée was constantly at his side in the hospital, and they eagerly discussed wedding plans as though his illness were nothing more than a cold. Hugh knew that he would not recover and reluctantly seemed to accept the circumstances as a kind of payment for past deeds. He died on March 30, 1959, and was buried next to his mother, Belle, at Belcrest Memorial Park in Salem.[4]

Roy

As noted, Roy did not transition easily to prison life. Deep-seated psychological problems tortured his mind for years, and he became hopelessly antisocial. With diminishing mental capacity, he grew further apart from cellmate, Ray, and the real world. Roy was committed to the Oregon State Mental Hospital (where he had worked as an attendant in 1920 while Ray was in jail in Washington State). A prefrontal lobotomy performed in 1950 was not successful, and Roy grew steadily less cognitive.

There seemed to be only three things important to Roy in his simplified life: sodas, candy bars and playing pool (with no scoring). During one of their last visits, Ray gave Roy candy bars and a soda. Roy smiled with delight but did not speak. The next day, when an attendant asked Roy about his brother's visit, Roy slowly grinned and squealed, "Candy, Coke!" He did not mention having a visitor.[5] Roy "lived" a few more years at the mental hospital and then was moved into a nursing home. He died on June 17, 1983, and was buried next to his mother and Hugh at Belcrest Memorial Park.

RAY

Ray, like brother Hugh, decided to make the most of circumstances. Choosing to be contributory and productive in prison, he came to enjoy teaching (serving as a Spanish language instructor for other inmates). Ray was a frequent contributor to Hugh's prison magazine, *Shadows*. He studied French and read endlessly. He and Hugh discovered that they both had artistic abilities. While Hugh mastered the printing arts and trade, Ray began to paint. His work was popular, and he sold paintings inside the prison hobby shop and outside the penitentiary.

Attorney Noreen Kelly took a legal direction similar to what she used to free Hugh. She was able to gain parole for Ray effective October 26, 1961. After nearly forty-five years of running, hiding and confinement, he faced significant adjustment to life on the outside, just as Hugh had. With his notoriety, Ray understandably was an introvert. Friends were able to find a part-time janitorial job for him sixty miles away at the University of Oregon in Eugene. They felt that the mileage buffer between Salem and Eugene would afford him measures of security and privacy. With the help of friends, he found a small rental house near the university. It needed work, but Ray found it comfortable and was grateful for his new home.

Not long after moving to Eugene, Ray wandered into a neighborhood church, where the congregation welcomed him. Although he had developed his own set of philosophical and religious beliefs, he seemed to fit right into this friendly little church. Members hauling in building materials and repairing Ray's house did much to bring him out of his introversion. As he became braver and more sociable, Ray taught painting and Spanish, usually to seniors at nearby community centers. Ray felt that, given alternatives, he was living a pretty good life. He had avoided the hangman's noose, left the penitentiary through parole and found ways to achieve and contribute.

However, Ray wanted more: he wanted to clear his name. He seemed to accept that history cannot be rewritten but felt that it could be reinterpreted. The crime was committed decades earlier, and now many folks, citing Ray's excellent record, found sympathy for him. His policeman-author friend in Portland, John Howard, and other supporters who felt Ray had paid the price for his crime, persistently lobbied Governor Tom McCall on Ray's behalf. During November 1972, the governor bowed to public persuasion and commuted Ray's two consecutive life terms. With cameras rolling, Ray met the governor in his office, and they each gave a short speech about the other's accomplishments. Ray thanked the governor for the commutation and left the meeting feeling like a free man ("commuting" his sentence allowed Ray to travel without supervision).

October 11, 1973, marked a half-century since the Tunnel 13 tragedy. Earlier that fall, two of Portland's news media began work on projects to recognize the infamous crime: *Oregon Journal* staff writer Jack Pement's "Murder on the Gold Special" and KGW-TV commentator and narrator Richard Ross's *DeAutremont the Train Robber—DeAutremont the Man* documentary. They negotiated that each would involve Ray to a degree, but as they got into the projects, problems arose: the number of people involved made Ray uncomfortable, affecting his health and participation. At one point, Ray wondered if he really wanted to relive the horrific crime. His doctor ordered a week of bed rest. His health improved, and John Howard convinced Ray that his participation would be an important historical contribution. As a compromise, the *Oregon Journal* and KGW-TV agreed to work together on the project. What resulted were a twenty-five-thousand-word feature article presented in twelve parts and a fifty-five-minute video documentary. Very professional, neither one glamorized the crime.[6]

Ray lived the rest of his life simply and peacefully. He died in a Eugene care facility on December 20, 1984.

VERNE

If there was a "different" DeAutremont, one of Belle's five sons who was a law-abiding contributor to society, it was her oldest son, Verne. Eager to avoid any connection to his brothers' crime, Verne sought an anonymous, quiet life. That did not come easily, as his name and aviation career were too prominent.

Verne came to Oregon about the same time as Ray and Roy. All were looking for work in the lumber industry and were disappointed that wages were so meager. The difference between the brothers was that Verne saved his earnings, while the twins spent theirs exploring opportunities to launch crime careers. They had decided that a life of crime would be much more appealing than working for a living. When together at Christmas of 1922, Ray recruited Hugh to join the twins in planning a train robbery sometime after Hugh would graduate high school in June. Young Hugh was eager to join his big brothers in an exciting crime caper. When Ray offered the same opportunity to Verne—and Verne realized he was serious—he replied in no uncertain terms that he wanted no part in a crime.[7]

The holdup and murders occurred in spite of Verne, and suddenly there was the shame of the brothers' names on hundreds of thousands of reward posters. Following an extensive manhunt, Hugh was arrested in Manila in February 1927. Certain that he was innocent, parents Paul and Belle attended Hugh's trial and were in Jacksonville when the twins were arrested in early June and returned from Ohio. Shortly thereafter, the three brothers confessed to save their lives. Paul was inconsolable, unable to deal with the realities of the crime and the family's circumstances. Also grieving but still in control, Belle cabled Verne in New Mexico, telling him to sell the store and come to Salem—she wanted to be as close as possible to her sons in the penitentiary. While Verne settled their affairs in New Mexico, Belle found and bought the "Alexandria," a boardinghouse on Salem's Chemeketa Street.

Because little is known about Verne, it is not clear how he advanced from a choke-setter in the woods to an aviation entrepreneur during the decades following the 1920s. Verne learned to fly at Portland's Swan Island airport from famous instructor "Tex" Rankin and then worked for Rankin Air Service as a flight instructor. In later years, he told friends that he had flown contract air mail, probably out of Portland.

Belle asked Verne to move to Salem and help her with the boardinghouse. He did, and there he met aviation master mechanic Lee Eyerly. Eyerly had invented several flight simulators, like the "Whiffle Hen" and "Orientator," which he bragged would make it affordable for anyone to learn to fly.

Eyerly discovered that his flight simulators could be adapted to safe, fun carnival rides, like his "Loop-O-Plane" in 1933. In spite of the Great Depression, some folks still had means, and almost overnight, anything connected with aviation became popular. Fueling this love affair was Lindbergh's crossing of the Atlantic solo in the *Spirit of St. Louis* in May 1927—during Hugh DeAutremont's trial.

Eyerly soon had more orders for simulators and amusement rides than he could handle. He needed someone he could trust to assist with the business, and Verne DeAutremont seemed to fill the bill. Verne worked for Eyerly during the 1930s and sold flying lessons on the side.

With the Second World War looming, the demand for pilot training skyrocketed, and Verne found himself instructing with almost no time off. When nonmilitary flying was restricted to within three hundred miles of the coast, many flight training schools were forced to move farther inland. Verne packed a bag and set out for Bend, Oregon.[8] He became an acclaimed flight instructor, but his weight was a problem: he had been putting on pounds for years, and the young cadets complained that he was so big they had to learn to fly the J-3 Cubs twice: once with and once without Verne's considerable weight in the backseat.[9]

The U.S. Army Air Corps conducted its own training at the Salem Airport during the war. At one time, the air corps had thirty-five trainer aircraft parked along the fence. After the war, the airport was rehabilitated and renamed McNary Field.

During that period, Verne experienced a pair of life changes. First, he lost his beloved mother, Belle, in February 1945. As close as they were, adjusting was a difficult challenge for Verne. The second change, an opportunity, helped Verne deal with Belle's death. After the war, flying was more popular than ever. Discharged soldiers and sailors, pockets full of GI Bill money, eagerly sought flight training. Some bought airplanes, and Verne capitalized on the GI Bill. With the help of his small inheritance from Belle, he built a full-service aviation center in Salem, DeAutremont Aviation, offering instruction, sales, service and maintenance.

When the air corps left the airport, earlier tenants came back, vying for hangar space and facilities. Verne was able to recover stashes of old airplane parts and service manuals. For years, it was said if one needed parts or manuals for old airplanes, Verne had them, going back to the early 1930s.

Whether or not he was willing to accept it, Verne was a DeAutremont, with demons to wrestle. He had less and less contact with his father Paul's family in Eugene. He visited Hugh and the twins in the penitentiary, but less often over time. He was heard to say at least once that he would just as soon have nothing to do with one or more of his relatives. Verne's "family" became the large circle of his airport friends: instructors, pilots, mechanics, airport employees and friends who knew nothing about flying but loved being around Verne. These were the morning and afternoon coffee regulars who socialized at the airport's Flight Deck restaurant and talked about anything and everything, especially aviation and airplanes. Knowing that his old friends respected him, Verne occasionally discussed the Tunnel 13 crime and his brothers. Sometimes there were lighter moments, like the morning the Marion County sheriff stormed into the Flight Deck, demanding that pilots stop taking off from Runway 34 over the penitentiary.

"You're flying too low, and we think you're droppin' stuff to the DeAutremonts—this has gotta stop!" The sheriff also complained to Warden Cupp's office, but there is no evidence that pilots gave up using the airport's long runway.[10]

The economy after the war years was like one of Eyerly's carnival rides. It teased Verne into developing his ultramodern flight center, but the good years didn't last. DeAutremont Aviation suffered declines in flight training and maintenance.

Since Verne normally spent very little money, it was difficult for friends to judge when he went from rich to poor. When his car stopped running, he stopped driving. Friends noticed that Verne called cabs to get to and from the airport. Several friends, maybe half a dozen, began offering him car rides, and he would ask if they could stop at the grocery store on the way home. Sadly, Verne also stopped flying, even his beloved Piper Cub. Friends occasionally offered him plane rides, but with age and poor health, he grew less comfortable in an airplane.

Verne made friends easily, but he had no personal life: he was always at the airport, somewhere in the hangar or among stacks of paper on his desk. He usually took his meals at the Flight Deck, and sometimes during the day, he would be seen sitting at the bar, nursing a milkshake.

Verne sold a lot of aviation gas using an ancient tank truck that had to be hand-cranked to start and pump fuel. He was getting older, just like the truck. Aviation and the airport were changing. One friend remembered the time, late in Verne's life, when a group of young entrepreneurs gained a foothold at the airport and sought changes that would have put Verne out of business and out of their way. However, they miscalculated who stood where in friendship and respect circles. A public hearing was scheduled at city hall, and the room was packed with pilots, officials and Verne's friends. Some of the changes were enacted, but not before Verne was safely "grandfathered." The whippersnappers slunk out of the room with their tails between their legs.[11]

Verne never married, remembering how his parents argued constantly. If that was "family life," he wanted none of it. Aviation and his friends at the airport afforded him a better life. If he had his occasional curmudgeonly moments, he also had warmth and generosity that made up for shortcomings. A friend helping Verne with paperwork one day discovered that he was a very generous donor to several Native American relief efforts. This was a passion, but one that he did not talk about.[12]

Honest and honorable as Verne was, he had a few rehearsed answers for dealing with embarrassing questions (and only trusted friends were allowed such conversation). When asked why he didn't visit his family much, he answered matter-of-factly that they had destroyed his mother's life. When asked why he didn't go along or try to stop the holdup, he retorted that his brothers wouldn't allow it because he was the youngest. In fact, Verne was the *oldest* brother. He was born in 1899, the twins in 1900, Hugh in 1904 and Lee in 1907. These explanations seemed the easiest way to avoid or end an unpleasant conversation.

Verne died in a Salem nursing home on March 13, 1977, and rests at Belcrest Memorial Park with his beloved mother Belle, twins Ray and Roy and brother Hugh.

PAUL

Paul was not the worst husband or father imaginable, but he had shown that he was restless, intense and sometimes foolish. Whether seeking opportunity or just trying to avoid poverty, he moved his growing family from Iowa to Arkansas, Colorado, New Mexico, back to Colorado and then back to New Mexico. With each move, he exposed Belle and their young family to serious dangers and challenges. It was nearly a miracle that Paul's cattlemen enemies in New Mexico did not kill the family.

There were occasional good times, but they could not begin to make up for their constant bickering and fighting. When the hostility became unbearable, Ray and Roy left home. With the family breaking up, it is surprising that the boys and parents still shared feelings of love and devotion. For instance, Ray was defensive of Paul when he was cheated by middlemen and harangued by cattlemen. On their own in Oregon, the brothers pooled their meager resources to take care of one another, and they tried to help Paul and Belle when they could. Roy reflected on family loyalties, noting that "after saying goodbye to Ray, I went back to Salem with Dad and he needed my help and mother living in New Mexico needed my help. I could not help them both so I helped Dad. I worked for him to help him support his family and back in New Mexico there was a mother there needing more help."[13]

To report, as some have, merely that Paul divorced Belle, remarried, moved to Oregon and opened a barbershop understates history. In fact, Paul was making decisions that were life-changing for many. As noted, Ray and Roy couldn't stand their parents' fighting and left the family's Lakewood home in 1916 (Ray first and then Roy shortly thereafter). Also worn down by the hostility, Paul considered opportunities for his own escape. Returning to Colorado had appeal, but a more interesting opportunity came along.

Francisco "Pancho" Villa was waging civil war in Mexico, and there was a fear that, in a show of strength, he would cross the border and bring death and destruction to the U.S. border states. Fighting Mexican insurgents sounded better than fighting with Belle, so Paul joined the New Mexico National Guard.

Villa did ride north. On March 9, he and about 500 revolutionists invaded tiny Columbus, New Mexico. About 100 Mexicans and 17 Americans died in the attack. President Wilson and Major General John Pershing mobilized all state National Guard units and declared the "Mexican Punitive Expedition." By the end of July, 112,000 guardsmen had mobilized, including Paul's New Mexico Field Artillery Battery A. His service was not particularly noteworthy, and Paul mustered out of the guard with the rank of private at the conclusion of the Punitive Expedition in March 1917. The headstone on Paul's grave honors him as a veteran.[14]

Returning home to Lakewood, Paul did not adjust well or find the life he thought he was entitled to. When spring came, he left home and traveled north to the Cripple Creek area of Colorado. In May, Paul divorced Belle.[15] Spending the next year and a half between Colorado and Union County, Wyoming, he fell into an old routine: whenever he couldn't find work as a barber or wallpaper hanger, he moved on, generally west. During that time, Paul met Nellie Guard (eleven years younger than he), her two-year-old twins, Ivan and Inez Carter, and Frank Case, a four- or five-year-old nephew she had taken in. Nellie and Paul were married in the Lincoln County Courthouse in Kemmerer, Wyoming, on August 19, 1918.[16]

Paul must not have found a job to his liking around Kemmerer, because he moved his new family west to Soda Springs, Idaho, that fall. This is interesting because it speaks to Ray's relationship with his father in that Ray's draft card shows as his permanent address Paul's address in Soda Springs. At the time, Ray worked as a teamster, hauling coal out of Dines, Wyoming, for the Colony Coal Company. He was not wandering around the country aimlessly but rather was following and staying close to Paul. However, with Paul having two families now, there was a variety of uncomfortable feelings. Draft cards of the older boys help locate them during that time. Cards issued in September 1918 show Ray in Soda Springs, Verne a laborer at home in Lakewood and Roy a barber in Oklahoma City.[17] At ages fourteen and eleven, Hugh and Lee were still at home in Lakewood.

Although he left no discernable tracks, it is likely that Paul barbered briefly in Soda Springs before packing up his new family and heading west to Oregon's Willamette Valley. Paul operated a barbershop in Salem at the time Ray was arrested for IWW membership. The boys' confessions mention Ray visiting Paul's house in Salem at least once before his arrest.

In October 1921, Nellie gave birth in Salem to Charlie ("Chuck"), her only child by Paul and his sixth son.

Paul was devastated when the tunnel holdup criminals were identified as the DeAutremont brothers. He took brief comfort in believing that there had been a mistake—surely the boys had just taken new jobs in a logging camp somewhere. But when the three were captured and decided to confess to stay alive, Paul was crushed, overcome by emotion. Unable to fully grasp what was happening around him, Paul's conversation was sometimes nonsensical. Some felt that no father should have to endure the inconsolable grief that burdened Paul, but not everyone felt sorry for him. Mary Smith, who attended grade school with the twins in New Mexico, countered in a letter years later, "I knew these boys—they were bright boys and their mother saw they looked well kept, for the father contributed little."

After the trial, Paul took his new family back home to Eugene and tried to keep them out of the limelight as best he could. Brief marital problems brought on by the stress of family tragedy made that difficult.[18] A broken man who never would get beyond the pain of bad choices, Paul died in Eugene in November 1953.

BELLE

If Paul symbolized hopeless frustration and failure in the tragic DeAutremont story, then Belle represented perseverance and hope. She was a scrapper like Paul, but while he tended to flee hostility, Belle stayed and tried to work things out. That did not always work, and Paul divorced Belle in 1917. The three older boys having left home, it was not easy for her to make ends meet. A proud woman, it was hard for her to ask her sons to come home and help put food on the table for the younger brothers.

As if she did not have enough grief in her life, she learned in March 1927 that between the times of Hugh's capture and trial, her youngest son, Lee, had been shot and killed in Texas. Belle took Lee home for burial in Lakewood and then traveled alone to Jacksonville to support Hugh, about to stand trial. The emotions of Hugh's capture and Lee's death were enough to drive any mother to the edge, but Belle hung on.

The trial was not easy on the mother of the Tunnel 13 murderers. Mary Greiner Kelly pointed out some of the challenges Belle faced: "And I made a good friend out of his [Hugh's] mother, who was a sweet little woman. I couldn't see why she was kicked around like she was. A lot of people said, 'Ohhh, there's his mother!'"[19] The interviewer asked Mary if Belle really was "kicked around." "Well," she responded, "kind of sub rosa [secretly], but she could hear some of those snide cracks, you know. She was a very sensitive little thing."

Mary related that a couple living on Crater Lake Avenue in Medford took in and provided for Belle while she attended the trial in Jacksonville. Mary was so impressed by that act of kindness that it inspired her to go to the home in evenings to visit and cheer up Belle. Mary said that she and Belle remained good friends until Belle died.[20]

What held Belle together early in the trial was her conviction that Hugh was innocent and soon would be proven so. When the brothers confessed to the heinous crime, Belle was as devastated as Paul, but she mustered her strength and did what she had to do to help her sons. She wired Verne in Lakewood, instructing him to sell the store for her. In the mean time, she set out to find a boardinghouse in Salem where she would be close to her boys in the penitentiary. She bought the "Alexandria" on Chemeketa Street. This would be home for Belle and Verne for the rest of their lives. Making the best of circumstances until the end, Belle died in Salem in February 1945 and was interred at Belcrest Memorial Park. Mary added, "I corresponded with [Belle] for a long time. Then she came out and stayed near the kids in the penitentiary. And I saw her up there. She was a loyal little mother."[21]

HAZEL

That young Hazel would marry and live with "Elmer Goodwin" for nearly two years, never suspecting that he was the infamous Ray DeAutremont, perhaps entitles her to the distinction of the "most naïve" character of the story.

The Sprouse family was enamored of "Elmer," this handsome stranger, so bright and conversant. Hazel's father gladly consented to give her hand in marriage. With reward posters seemingly everywhere and showing reasonable likenesses of the brothers, it seems almost impossible that neither Hazel, family, friends nor neighbors recognized Ray or Roy. For nearly two

When Ray and Roy were fugitives living in Ohio, Ray was using the alias Elmer Goodwin and married to Hazel. Here she holds their infant son, Jackie Hugh. *U.S. Post Office Department.*

years before their arrest, Ray and Roy wandered the Ohio/Kentucky area looking for work or odd jobs. Hazel often traveled with Ray, and it was not unusual for the "youngsters" to make new friends. Life seemed good and even better with the birth of Jackie Hugh in June 1926. After a while, Ray and Roy carelessly allowed themselves to imagine that they might be able to hide there forever.

With Hugh's photo conspicuously missing from the latest wanted posters, Ray and Roy knew that he had been captured and that their time was coming soon. They were arrested in Steubenville on June 8, 1927, with only mild protest from Ray.

Stunned, Hazel stood in the Steubenville Police Station, holding Jackie Hugh tightly and struggling to understand what was going on. Who were these law officers, and why were they calling her husband Elmer "Ray DeAutremont?" When it was time to return to the holding cell, the officer led Ray away, and baby Jackie wailed loudly for his daddy. Ray imagined that his grief was as great as a person could feel. One wonders if he considered the families of the murdered trainmen and postal clerk.

The brothers were imprisoned in the Oregon State Penitentiary in June 1927. In spite of everything Hazel had been through as she followed the trial in newspapers, she remained loyal to the man who had deceived her so completely, the man she would have to learn to call "Ray."

Hazel scraped up the few dollars she could and then took the train to Oregon with Jackie Hugh. Having next to no resources, she asked Paul if she could stay with his family for a while. He reluctantly agreed, but that lasted only a short time. When she told the family that she intended to stay in Oregon to be close to Ray—naïve and impractical—they objected and convinced her to return to Ohio.[22] Naturally, Hazel's family was bitter toward Ray, but sadly, they could see how much she still loved him. Back in her parents' Lawrence County home, Hazel found that she was pregnant with another child. She decided that he would be named Raymond Charles DeAutremont Jr. and called Ray.

Hazel lived most of her life and brought up Jackie Hugh and Ray Jr. in the Ohio/Kentucky/West Virginia border area around Ironton, Ohio. In the mid-1950s, she divorced Ray after twenty-five years of penitentiary "marriage" and married Mr. Adkins in Ohio. He lived only a few years, leaving her a widow in the late 1950s. Tragedy struck again when son Ray Jr. died by his own hand in 1957. He had served as a U.S. Army corporal during the Korean War and evidently was unable to transition back to a normal life after combat. Jackie Hugh fared much better in adult life, retiring as superintendent of a plant in the Midwest and living until 1996. Hazel outlived both her husbands and both her sons. She died in a nursing home in Ironton in 2002 at age ninety-three.

NELLIE

Nellie was Paul's second wife and "second chance" in life. Before meeting her, he had given up his marriage, family and home and drifted west, hoping to start over. He met and married Nellie in Wyoming. With her twins and a nephew, Paul gained an instant second family.

Left: Born to Paul's second wife, Nellie, in 1921, Chuck DeAutremont (sometimes "Charlie" to the family) was a half-brother to Ray, Roy and Hugh. *Smith Family Collection and Stan Smith.*

Opposite: Three generations of DeAutremonts, circa 1947: Charlie, Steve and Paul. *Smith Family Collection and Stan Smith.*

Life was not easy for Nellie, especially with multiple families. With friction in the air, helping Dad's new wife was a tough assignment for the brothers. At a time when she needed more help, not more children, she gave birth to "Charlie" in October 1921. Their little Eugene bungalow on West Twentieth Street could barely shelter her family (a boarder, Miss Todd, provided some help to Nellie). If one of the older boys came to town and sought a bed for the night, there often was none. It was understandable that relationships sometimes were strained.

With Paul's sons' horrific crime at Tunnel 13, life became a nightmare for Nellie. All she wanted was anonymity and privacy so she could deal with the family tragedy. What she got was persistent hounding by media and hoards of the curious. Hazel's naïve conversations with anyone who cornered her were especially damaging, so family convinced Hazel to return home to Ohio and her parents.

Nellie's marriage to Paul was tested by the strain of tragedy and Paul's difficulty dealing with reality. Paul was sometimes publicly critical of Nellie. Over time, they were able to work out their marital problems.

Just as there was a particular closeness between Belle and son Verne and another between Hazel and Jackie Hugh, so, too, was there a closeness between Nellie and her youngest, "Charlie." A 1928 Eugene School District roster of "crippled" children lists Charlie (age seven).[23] Neither the purpose of the report nor the young boy's malady is remembered. What is known is that Charlie decided to trade his "crippled" status for awards of high achievement: superiority in athletics, academics and coaching. Charlie, like his half-brother Verne, was a DeAutremont who would achieve and contribute.

Nellie died in April 1969 and Charlie in January 2006.

Ray DeAutremont was right in saying that little variations make big differences in life, but he was wrong to profess that outcomes are predestined. The lives of the DeAutremonts did not have to be tragic. Verne and Charlie were brothers who showed that there are alternatives, choices and opportunities to live differently—opportunities to climb that other mountain.

finis
–conclusion of confession of Roy A. DeAutremont, June 23, 1927

NOTES

CHAPTER 1

1. Southern Pacific Lines Shasta Route Time Tables—May 10, 1923.
2. Robert Church letter to author re: Decks.
3. Diebert and Strapac, *Southern Pacific Company Steam Locomotive Compendium*, 214; Wright, *Southern Pacific Company Diagrams*, vol. 1, 106; Signor, *Southern Pacific's Shasta Division*, 59.
4. Wright, *Southern Pacific Company Diagrams*, vol. 1, 266, 269.
5. Johnson, "1923 Tunnel 13 Holdup Argument Solved," forum posts.
6. *Southern Pacific Bulletin*, "S.P. Men Slain in Train Hold-up," 10–11.
7. Whether a steam engine is serviced at the roundhouse or out on the road, its many moving parts require thorough, frequent lubrication. First, the roundhouse hostler or engineman checks the level of steam cylinder oil in the mechanical lubricator to ensure constant lubrication to the steam cylinders and air pumps. Next, he goes to each of the ten drive wheels and looks for any problems with the pad lubricators in their journals. Finding none, he lubes the "valve motion"—all the back-and-forth rods and linkage on both sides of the loco that transmit the pistons' motion to the drive wheels' rotation. As he works, he watches carefully for nuts, bolts, dragging equipment and anything out of place. Fahrenwald, *Running a Steam Locomotive*, vol. 2.
8. Signor, *Southern Pacific's Shasta Division*, 21.

9. Ainsworth, telephone interview, 11. This would allow him to use No. 3626's "independent brake" to slow that locomotive, but as a double-heading engine, it was isolated from the train braking system. Only the helper engine could control train braking in this configuration.

10. Ainsworth, author training, December 7, 2011, 5. Two glass tubes or "water glasses" (one on the engineer's side and one on the fireman's side) measured the critical water level in the loco's boiler. If the water in the boiler fell, for any reason, to a level that exposed the crown sheet, then the tremendous heat of the firebox would cause a catastrophic explosion. Downhill grades were critical: when a loco tipped forward, its water level on the crown sheet would fall.

11. Webber and Webber, *Siskiyou Line*, 175.

12. Southern Pacific Historical & Technical Society (hereafter SPH&TS), *Southern Pacific Passenger Cars*, vol. 3, 116.

13. Chipman, *Tunnel 13*, 1.

14. Jackson County Circuit Court, *State v. DeAutremont*, vol. 1, *Trial Testimony, Hugh DeAutremont Trial* (hereafter *Trial Testimony*), 118–35.

15. Ibid., 111–12.

16. Webber and Webber, *Oregon's Great Train Holdup*, 62.

17. *Trial Testimony*, 4.

18. From Southern Pacific Company (Pacific System), *Rules and Regulations of the Transportation Department*, August 1, 1907, Running Test Procedure ("running brake test"): "Test must be made as soon as speed of train is sufficient to prevent stalling. While using sufficient power to keep train stretched, apply train brakes with sufficient force to ascertain whether or not train brakes are operating properly. Engine brakes must be kept released during running test."

19. Signor, *Southern Pacific's Shasta Division*, 336–37.

CHAPTER 2

1. Hanson, "History of Williamsburg, Iowa."

2. *Williamsburg Journal Tribune*, "Charming Wedding."

3. This August 15, 1902 article from the *Journal* might suggest that Belle and her hens were settling into Mena in December 1901. Other excerpts state that Paul took a short business trip and sold the house during March

1902. With Belle caring for three toddlers, she could not have preceded Paul to Mena in December 1901. It is reasonable to assume that the DeAutremonts moved as a family to Mena after March 1902 and that Belle acquired busy, prolific hens after she moved.

4. Roy DeAutremont, "Confession," 1.
5. Chipman, *Tunnel 13*, 58.
6. Enders, "Wobblies Never Had a Good Foothold."
7. Chipman, *Tunnel 13*, 59–60.
8. Roy DeAutremont, "Confession," 7.
9. Sturholm and Howard, *All for Nothing*, 31.

CHAPTER 3

1. Chipman, *Tunnel 13*, 63.
2. Mangold, oral history interview with Harold Putnam, 1.
3. Ibid.
4. Google Earth Community, "Last Big Train Robbery, Tunnel 13," 4.
5. Miller, "Rogue Valley History," 6A.
6. Ibid.
7. Google Earth Community, "Last Big Train Robbery, Tunnel 13," 3–4.
8. Mangold, oral history interview with Harold Putnam, 2.
9. Roy DeAutremont, "Confession," 16.
10. Ibid.
11. Ibid., 18.
12. Ibid.

CHAPTER 4

1. Roy DeAutremont, "Confession," 19.
2. Pintarich, *Great & Minor Moments*, 237.
3. *Trial Testimony*, 238–39.
4. Roy DeAutremont, "Confession," 19–20.
5. Ibid., 39.

6. Ibid., 20; Ray DeAutremont, "Confession," 2.

7. Roy DeAutremont, "Confession," 39.

8. Engle, *Oral History Interview*, 1.

9. *Medford Mail Tribune*, "Hold Funeral Bandit Victim Here Monday." While many have misspelled his nickname "Coyle," obituaries and the family burial plot in Medford's IOOF Eastwood Cemetery show that both Johnson and one of his two deceased sons used the name "Coyl."

10. Roy DeAutremont, "Confession," 20.

11. Ibid.

12. Ibid.

13. Ray DeAutremont, "Confession," 2.

14. Ibis., 20–21.

15. Cadwalader and Bowerman, "Capture of the D'Autremont Brothers," 46.

16. *Trial Testimony*, 46.

17. Roy DeAutremont, "Confession," 21.

18. *Trial Testimony*, 10.

19. *Ashland Daily Tidings*, "Worst Murder Case," 45.

20. International Adventist Musicians Online, "Lawrence Eugene Claire Joers, 1–2.

21. *Trial Testimony*, 13.

22. Ibid., 14–15.

23. Ibid., 15.

24. Ibid., 52.

25. Hunter, diary entries October 11, 1923, and October 12, 1924.

Chapter 5

1. *Ashland Daily Tidings*, "Worst Murder Case," 1.

2. Roy DeAutremont, "Confession," 21.

3. Cadwalader and Bowerman, "Capture of the D'Autremont Brothers," 20.

4. Pement, "Murder on the Gold Special—Part 7," 12+.

5. Ibid.

6. Ibid.

7. Ibid., "Murder on the Gold Special—Part 6," 4.

8. Roy DeAutremont, "Confession," 22.
9. Chipman, *Tunnel 13*, 80–81.
10. Ibid., 28.
11. Roy DeAutremont, "Confession," 28.
12. Ibid., 28–29.
13. Ibid., 29.
14. *Eugene Register Guard*, "Detailed Confession," 1, 19.
15. *Medford Mail Tribune*, "Siskiyou Suspect in Philippines," 1.
16. Pement, "Murder on the Gold Special—Part 10," 4.
17. DeNevi, *Western Train Robberies*, 150.
18. Ibid.
19. Pement, "Murder on the Gold Special—Part 10," 4.
20. Ibid.
21. *Eugene Register Guard*, "Lee D'Autremont Shot in Accident," 1; *Eugene Register Guard*, "Lee DeAutremont Dies of Injuries," 1.
22. Eagleton, *On the Last Frontier*; Kerr and Donovan, *Destination Topolobampo*; *Texas State Board of Health Standard Certificate of Death (Form D)—#1075*
23. Chipman, *Tunnel 13*, 106.
24. Ibid.

Chapter 6

1. Cadwalader and Bowerman, "Capture of the D'Autremont Brothers," 21.
2. Ibid.
3. Ibid., 22.
4. Pement, "Murder on the Gold Special—Part 11," 4.
5. Ibid.
6. Cadwalader and Bowerman, "Capture of the D'Autremont Brothers," 22.
7. Chipman, *Tunnel 13*, 109.
8. Cadwalader and Bowerman, "Capture of the D'Autremont Brothers," 22.
9. Fattig, "Nothing Great About It," 1+.
10. Cadwalader and Bowerman, "Capture of the D'Autremont Brothers," 22.
11. *Trial Testimony*, 29.

12. Ibid., 26.

13. Cadwalader and Bowerman, "Capture of the D'Autremont Brothers," 66.

14. Ibid.

15. Sturholm, Howard and Shangle, *All for Nothing*, 148.

16. Chipman, *Tunnel 13*, 115.

17. Sturholm, Howard and Shangle, *All for Nothing*, 159.

18. Ibid., 157.

19. Cadwalader and Bowerman, "Capture of the D'Autremont Brothers," 67.

20. Sturholm, Howard and Shangle, *All for Nothing*, 158.

21 Cadwalader and Bowerman, "Capture of the D'Autremont Brothers," 68.

22. Pement, "Murder on the Gold Special—Part 11," 4.

23. Cadwalader and Bowerman, "Capture of the D'Autremont Brothers," 67.

24. Sturholm, Howard and Shangle, *All for Nothing*, 106.

25. Kelly, *Oral History Interview with Mary Kelly*, 19.

26. *Medford Mail Tribune*, "Death Penalty Demanded," 8.

27. Mangold and Mangold, *Oral History Interview with Ruth Schleigh*.

28. Cadwalader and Bowerman, "Capture of the D'Autremont Brothers," 68.

29. Ibid.

30. Ibid.

31. Sturholm, Howard and Shangle, *All for Nothing*, 162–63.

32. Cadwalader and Bowerman, "Capture of the D'Autremont Brothers," 69.

33. Ibid., 70.

34. Sturholm, Howard and Shangle, *All for Nothing*, 164.

35. Chipman, *Tunnel 13*, 120; Sturholm, Howard and Shangle, *All for Nothing*, 165.

36. Hugh DeAutremont, "Confession," 1; Kelly, *Oral History Interview with Mary Kelly*, 16.

37. *Medford Mail Tribune*, "Three D'Autremonts Confess," 1.

38. Hugh DeAutremont, "Confession," 1; Ray DeAutremont, "Confession," 3; Roy DeAutremont, "Confession," 42.

39. Pement, "Murder on the Gold Special—Part 11," 4.

40. Ibid.

41. Sturholm, Howard and Shangle, *All for Nothing*, 172.

42. Pement, "Murder on the Gold Special—Part 11," 4.
43. *Medford Mail Tribune*, "Three D'Autremonts Confess," 1.

Chapter 7

1. Pement, "Murder on the Gold Special—Part 12," 12.
2. Ibid.
3. Chipman, *Tunnel 13*, 133–34.
4. DeAutremont, Christmas card to Mary E. Smith; Hugh DeAutremont, letter to Mary E. Smith.
5. Pement, "Murder on the Gold Special—Part 12," 12.
6. Chipman, *Tunnel 13*, 134.
7. Ibid., 135.
8. Kelly, *Oral History Interview with Mary Kelly*, 21.
9. Jewett, "Mary Kelly Recalls Covering," A11.
10. Sturholm, Howard and Shangle, *All for Nothing*, 179–80.
11. Kelly, *Oral History Interview with Mary Kelly*, 21.
12. Chipman, *Tunnel 13*, 150–52.
13. McGraw, e-mail interview, December 1, 2011
14. Ibid., December 2, 2011
15. Ibid.
16. Ibid.
17. Ibid.
18. Ibid., December 3, 2011.
19. Ibid., December 2, 2011.

Chapter 8

1. Chipman, *Tunnel 13*, 137–39.
2. Ibid., 138.
3. McGraw, e-mail interview, December 3, 2011.
4. Stark, letter to Mary E. Smith.
5. Pement, "Murder on the Gold Special—Part 12," 12.

6. Marks, "DeAutremont's Story Due on TV Sunday," 7.

7. Roy DeAutremont, "Confession," 15.

8. *Bend Bulletin*, "Flight School Chooses Bend as Location," 1.

9. Morris, "Monday, September 10, 2007."

10. Bellows, telephone/e-mail interview, 2.

11. Lovell, telephone/e-mail interview.

12. Ibid.

13. Roy DeAutremont, "Confession," 7.

14. Daniel, "New Mexico's Participation," 1–3.

15. Cadwalader and Bowerman, "Capture of the D'Autremont Brothers," 21.

16. Ancestry.com, Western States Marriage Index, 1809–2011, 1–2.

17. Ancestry.com, World War I Draft Registration Cards.

18. *Medford Mail Tribune*, "Paul DeAutremont Asks for Divorce," 1.

19. Kelly, *Oral History Interview with Mary Kelly*, 8.

20. Ibid.

21. Ibid., 8–9.

22. Pement, "Murder on the Gold Special—Part 12," 12.

23. State of Oregon, Lane County School District No. 4, *Clerk's Census Report of Crippled Children*, 29.

BIBLIOGRAPHY

BOOKS

Allen, E.S., comp. and ed. *The Official Guide of the Railways, June 1916.* New York: National Railway Publication Company, 1916.

Artesia High School 1923 yearbook. Artesia, NM: self-published, 1923.

Block, Eugene. *Great Train Robberies of the West.* New York: Coward-McCann, 1959.

Buys, Christian J., Amy E. Taylor and C.R. Taylor. *Historic Ashland in Rare Photographs.* Lake City, CO: Western Reflections Publishing Company, 2010.

Chipman, Art. *Tunnel 13.* Medford, OR: Pine Cone Publishers, 1977.

Culp, Edward D. *Stations West: The Story of the Oregon Railways.* Caldwell, ID: Caxton Printer, 1972.

DeNevi, Don. *Western Train Robberies.* Surrey, BC: Hancock House Publishing, 1994.

Diebert, Timothy S., and Joseph Strapac. *Southern Pacific Company Steam Locomotive Compendium.* Huntington Beach, CA: Shade Tree Books, 1987.

Dill, Tom, and Larry Castle, eds. *Southern Pacific Railroad Images Ashland Oregon.* N.p., n.d.

Dunscomb, Guy L., Donald K. Dunscomb and Robert A. Pecotich. *Southern Pacific Steam Pictorial.* Vol. 2. USA, 1999.

Eagleton, Nancy Ethie. *On the Last Frontier: A History of Upton County, Texas*. El Paso, TX: Western Press, 1971.

Joers, Lawrence E.C., and Dick Pintarich, eds. "The Siskiyou Train Robbery." *Great and Minor Moments in Oregon History*, New Oregon Publishers, Inc., Portland, OR, 2008.

Kerr, John Leeds, and Frank Donovan. *Destination Topolobampo: The Kansas City, Mexico & Orient Railway*. San Marino, CA: Golden West, 1968.

LaPlante, Margaret. *The DeAutremont Brothers: America's Last Great Train Robbery*. N.p., 2009.

Livingston, Jill. *That Ribbon of Highway III: Highway 99 through the Pacific Northwest*. Klamath River, CA: Living Gold Press, 2003.

Perry, Arthur Gordon. "The Life and Crimes of the Deautremont Brothers." N.p., circa 1930.

Pintarich, Dick. *Great & Minor Moments in Oregon History*. Portland, OR: New Oregon Publishers Inc., 2003.

Signor, John R. *Rails in the Shadow of Mt. Shasta*. San Diego, CA: Howell-North Books, 1982.

————. *Southern Pacific's Shasta Division: Over a Century of Railroading in the Shadow of Mt. Shasta*. Wilton and Berkeley, CA: Signature Press, 2000.

Southern Pacific Historical & Technical Society, ed. *Diagrams, Common Standard Passenger Train Cars Southern Pacific Lines as of March 1, 1933*. N.p.: self-published, n.d.

————. *Southern Pacific Passenger Cars*. Vol. 3. *Head End Equipment*. N.p.: self-published, 2007.

Sturholm, Larry, John Howard and Robert D. Shangle. *All for Nothing: The True Story of the Last Great American Train Robbery*. Portland, OR: BLS Publishing, 1976.

Webber, Bert, and Margie Webber. *Oregon's Great Train Holdup: Bandits Murder 4—Didn't Get a Dime*. Medford, OR: Webb Research Group, 1988.

————. *The Siskiyou Line*. Medford, OR: Webb Research Group, 2002.

Webber, Bert, comp. and ed. *Oregon's Great Train Holdup: The DeAutremont Case Number 57893-D*. Fairfield, WA: Ye Galleon Press, 1974.

Williams, Brad. *Legendary Outlaws of the West*. New York: David McKay Company, 1976.

Wright, Richard K., ed. *Southern Pacific Company Diagrams of Locomotives and Tenders*. Vol. 1. Oakhurst, CA: Wright Enterprises, 1973.

Yuskavitch, Jim. *Outlaw Tales of Oregon*. Guilford, CT: Globe Pequot Press, 2006.

ARTICLES

Aplin, Glenn. "The Great Oregon Train Holdup." *Pacific Northwest Forum* 5, no. 1 (Winter 1980).

Ashland Daily Tidings. "Worst Murder Case Annals of North West." October 12, 1923.

Bend Bulletin. "Flight School Chooses Bend as Location." September 19, 1942.

Cadwalader, A.B., and Dan Bowerman. "The Capture of the D'Autremont Brothers." *True Detective Mysteries*, March 1928 and April 1928.

Enders, John. "Wobblies Never Had a Good Foothold in Area." *Mail Tribune*, March 23, 1989.

Eugene Register Guard. "Detailed Confession Is Given in Cell by Hugh." June 23, 1927.

———. "Lee D'Autremont Shot in Accident in City in Texas." February 28, 1927.

———. "Lee DeAutremont Dies of Injuries." March 1, 1927.

———. "Vern DeAutremont Here." August 24, 1927.

Fattig, Paul. "Nothing Great About It." *Medford Mail Tribune*, October 11, 1998.

Jewett, Dick. "Mary Kelly Recalls Covering Nation's 'Story of the Year' as a Cub Reporter." *Medford Mail Tribune*, October 29, 1981.

Marks, Arnold. "DeAutremont's Story Due on TV Sunday." *Oregon Journal*, September 28, 1973, 7.

Medford Mail Tribune. "Death Penalty Demanded." June 20, 1927.

———. "Hold Funeral Bandit Victim Here Monday." March 13, 1923.

———. "Paul DeAutremont Asks for Divorce." November 5, 1927.

———. "Siskiyou Suspect in Philippines." February 12, 1927. 1+.

———. "Three D'Autremonts Confess, Tell Complete Story of Heinous Crime." June 23, 1927.

Miller, Bill. "Rogue Valley History: Harold Putnam, Growing Up on the Pass." *Senior Views*, June 2008.

Pement, Jack. "Murder on the Gold Special—Part 1." *Oregon Journal*, September 25, 1973.

———. "Murder on the Gold Special—Part 2." *Oregon Journal*, September 26, 1973.

———. "Murder on the Gold Special—Part 3." *Oregon Journal*, September 27, 1973.

———. "Murder on the Gold Special—Part 4." *Oregon Journal*, September 28, 1973.

———. "Murder on the Gold Special—Part 5." *Oregon Journal*, October 1, 1973.

———. "Murder on the Gold Special—Part 6." *Oregon Journal*, October 2, 1973.

———. "Murder on the Gold Special—Part 7." *Oregon Journal*, October 3, 1973.

———. "Murder on the Gold Special—Part 8." *Oregon Journal*, October 4, 1973.

———. "Murder on the Gold Special—Part 9." *Oregon Journal*, October 5, 1973.

———. "Murder on the Gold Special—Part 10." *Oregon Journal*, October 8, 1973.

———. "Murder on the Gold Special—Part 11." *Oregon Journal*, October 9, 1973.

———. "Murder on the Gold Special—Part 12." *Oregon Journal*, October 10, 1973.

[Portland] *Oregonian*. "Life Outside Proves Brief." March 31, 1959.

Southern Pacific Bulletin. "S.P. Men Slain in Train Hold-up." November 1923.

Thompson, Peter, and Jerry Tippens. "Astute Detective Work Turns Up Robbers' Identity." *Oregon Journal*, August 14, 1963.

Williamsburg Journal Tribune. "A Charming Wedding." November 12, 1897.

VIDEOS

DeAutremont the Train Robber—DeAutremont the Man. Available on CD-ROM. Portland, OR: KGW-TV, 1972.

End of an Era. Available on CD-ROM. Eugene, OR: Direct Hit Productions, Peacepipe Videography, 1972.

Fahrenwald, Andy. *Running a Steam Locomotive Vol. 2*. SMP Video Publishing Inc., 2005.

Passenger Locomotive Road Operation. Available on CD-ROM: SMP Video Publishing, 1992.

Web Sources

Ancestry.com. "Census Place: Salem, Marion, Oregon; Roll: 1948; Page: 5B; Enumeration District: 56; Image 113.0." United States of America, Bureau of the Census, Fifteenth Census of the United States, 1930. http://search.ancestry.com/cgi.bin/ssedll?h=109454291&db=1930usfedcen&indiv=try. Unable to access a free source for this census info. Available through Ancestry.com.

———. "Ray Charles DeAutremont." World War I Draft Registration Cards. United States Selective Service System, World War I Selective Service System Draft Registration Cards, 1917–1918. M1509, 4,582 rolls. Washington, D.C.: National Archives and Records Administration. Imaged from Family History Library microfilm. http://search.ancestry.com/cgi-bin/sse.dll?h=24238398&db=WW1draft&indiv=try. Unable to access a free source for this draft card info. Available through Ancestry.com.

———. "Roy Andrew DeAutremont." World War I Draft Registration Cards. World War I Draft Registration Cards. United States Selective Service System, World War I Selective Service System Draft Registration Cards, 1917–1918. M1509, 4,582 rolls. Washington, D.C.: National Archives and Records Administration. Imaged from Family History Library microfilm. http://search.ancestry.com/cgi-bin/sse.dll?h=24096812&db=WW1draft&indiv=try. Unable to access a free source for draft card info. Available through Ancestry.com.

———. "Verne Paul DeAutremont." World War I Draft Registration Cards. World War I Draft Registration Cards. United States Selective Service System, World War I Selective Service System Draft Registration Cards, 1917–1918. M1509, 4,582 rolls. Washington, D.C.: National Archives and Records Administration. Imaged from Family History Library microfilm. http://search.ancestry.com/cgi-bin/sse.dll?h=24096813&db=WW1draft&indiv=try. Unable to access a free source for this draft card info. Available through Ancestry.com.

———. Western States Marriage Index, 1809–2011 (database online). Brigham Young University–Idaho. Unable to access a free source for this marriage index. Available through Ancestry.com.

City of Portland, Oregon. "1929 Swan Island Airport." http://www.portlandonline.com/auditor/index.cfm?print=1&a=24729&c=27928.

Daniel, Karen Stein. "New Mexico's Participation in the Mexican Punitive Expedition: Prelude to World War I." New Mexico Genealogist, September 2005. http://www.nmgs.org/artNM-WWI.htm.

Dollarhide, William W. "Jesse Dollarhide and Descendants through Five Generations: A Pioneer Family of Jackson County, Oregon." Dollarhide Family Website, July 1999. http://www.dollarhide.org/histjesse.htm.

Google Earth Community. "The Last Big Train Robbery, Tunnel 13." http:// productforums.google.com/forum/#!msg/gec-history-illustrated-moderated/zARmXRF5Srg/lRBWSEBDlW0J.

Hanson, Loretta. "History of Williamsburg, Iowa." Williamsburg, Iowa, 2007. http://www.williamsburgiowa.org/History.html.

International Adventist Musicians Online. "Lawrence Eugene Claire Joers." http://www.iamaonline.com/Bio/Lawrence_E.C._Joers.htm.

Johnson, Tony. "Nostalgia & History > 1923 Tunnel 13 Holdup Argument Solved." Trainorders.com, November 30, 2005. http://www.trainorders. com/discussion/read.php?11,1048796.

Morris, Robert L. "Monday, September 10, 2007." WWII.HumpPilot. http://wwiihumppilot.blogspot.com/2007/09/chapter-2-life-tales-of-wwii-hump-pilot_10.html.

Oregon Aviation Historical Society. "1998: John G. 'Tex' Rankin." http:// oregonaviation.org/hall-of-fame.

Smithsonian Institute National Postal Museum. "Robberies." http://www. postalmuseum.si.edu/exhibits/2c1d_robberies.html.

LETTERS

Church, Dr. Robert J.. Letter to author, June 23, 2013. Organized and stored in author's collection.

DeAutremont, Hugh. Christmas card to Mary E. Smith, n.d. Organized and stored in author's collection.

———. Letter to Mary E. Smith, April 13, 1947. Organized and stored in author's collection.

Hunter, Mary L. Pages from diary, October 12, 1927. Organized and stored in author's collection.

Putnam, Diane. Letter to the author, December 25, 2011. Organized and stored in author's collection.

Stark, Gary L. Letter to Mary E. Smith, May 19, 1972. Organized and stored in author's collection.

ORAL HISTORIES, INTERVIEWS AND TRAINING

Ainsworth, Bill. Author training and instruction, Central Point, OR, December 7, 2011.

————. Author training and instruction, Central Point, OR, November 14, 2011.

————. Author training and instruction, Central Point, OR, November 28, 2011.

————. Telephone interview, August 1, 2011.

Baum, Gerald. *Oral History Interview with Hugh F. Barron.* Tape cassette OH#16. Jacksonville: Southern Oregon Historical Society, April 1, 1975.

Bellows, Joe. Telephone/e-mail/U.S. mail interview with author, January 5, 2012.

Engle, Fred S. *Oral History Interview with Fred S. Engle.* Tape cassette OH#40. Jacksonville: Southern Oregon Historical Society, November 1, 1976.

Glenn, John. Telephone/e-mail interview with author, January 6, 2012.

Hellie, Bill. Telephone/e-mail interview with author, January 3, 2012.

Holmes, Mark. Telephone/e-mail interview with author, January 3, 2012.

Jensen, Barbara and Joy Beebe. Telephone/e-mail interview with author, January 3, 2012.

Kelly, Mary Greiner. *Oral History Interview with Mary Kelly.* Tape cassette OH#148. Jacksonville: Southern Oregon Historical Society.

Kinney, Jim. Telephone/e-mail interview with author, January 3, 2012.

Lambert, Greg. Telephone/e-mail interview with author, January 3, 2012.

Lovell, Hadley. Telephone/e-mail interview with author, January 9, 2012.

Mangold, Scott. Oral history interview with Harold Putnam, April 29, 2009.

Mangold, Scott, and Lori Mangold. *Oral History Interview with Ruth Schleigh.* Tape cassette of oral history. Central Point, OR, October 20, 2011.

McGraw, Noreen Kelly. E-mail interviews with author, November 27, 2011; December 1, 2011; December 2, 2011; December 3, 2011.

Wenger, Charles. Telephone/e-mail interview with author, January 9, 2012.

MAPS

Ashland Quadrangle [NIMA1468 II NW-Series V892], topographic map. *7.5-Minute Series.* U.S. Department of Interior Geological Survey, 1996.
Emigrant Lake Quadrangle [42122-B5-TF-024], topographic map. *7.5-Minute Series.* U.S. Department of Interior Geological Survey, 1983.
Mt. Ashland Quadrangle [NIMA 1468 II SW-Series V892], topographic map. *7.5-Minute Series.* U.S. Department of Interior Geological Survey, 1998.
Siskiyou Pass, Oreg.-Calif. [42122-A5-TF-024], topographic map. *7.5-Minute Series.* U.S. Department of Interior Geological Survey, 1983.

REPORTS AND SCHEDULES

DeAutremont, Hugh. "Confession." *Trial of Hugh DeAutremont.* Medford, OR: County of Jackson, June 23, 1927.
DeAutremont, Ray. "Confession." Medford, OR: County of Jackson, June 23, 1927.
DeAutremont, Roy. "Confession." Medford, OR: County of Jackson, June 23, 1927.
Jackson County Circuit Court. *State v. DeAutremont.* Vol. 1. *Trial Testimony, Hugh DeAutremont Trial.* Jacksonville, OR, June 1927.
Southern Pacific Company Archival Files of the Shasta Division, Dunsmuir, California.
Southern Pacific Company (Pacific System). *Rules and Regulations of the Transportation Department,* August 1, 1907.
Southern Pacific Lines Shasta Route Time Tables—May 10, 1923, Dunsmuir, California.
State Highway Commission Biennial Report, 1917–1918. Salem: Oregon Department of Transportation, 1919.
State of Oregon, Lane County School District No. 4. *Clerk's Census Report of Crippled Children,* 1928. Lane County, Oregon Department of Education.
Texas State Board of Health Standard Certificate of Death (Form D)—#1075. Texas Bureau of Vital Statistics, March 2, 1927.

INDEX

ABOUT THE AUTHOR

A native of the Pacific Northwest, Scott was born in Seattle, raised in Portland and graduated Willamette University in Salem with a degree in economics. Although a U.S. Air Force veteran and a manager during most of his thirty-five-year airline career, Scott professes always to have been more interested in trains than planes. A lover of history in general—and southern Oregon being rich in history—Scott knew that he and wife, Lori, would have to retire there. Since moving to the Medford area, Scott has served on the board of the Ashland Historic Railroad Museum and is a volunteer researcher at the Southern Oregon Historical Society. Besides being a history buff, Scott is an active model railroader when time permits.

Photo by Dawna Curler.